Recipes: Wines and Spirits

Contents

Goods of ...

TIME-LIFE BOOKS, NEW YORK

Equipment and Techniques

OLD-FASHIONED	STEM COCKTAIL	HIGHBALL
6 to 10 ounces	3 to 4½ ounces	8 to 12 ounces

Glasses for the Bar

Silhouetted above are five types of standard bar glasses and one all-purpose wine glass, which are called for in this booklet's recipes for drinks. In recent years there has been a trend toward larger glasses—the king-sized old-fashioned glass is an example—and a range of capacities is suggested for the glasses shown. A larger cocktail or highball, however, allows more time for the liquid to become warm, for the taste to flatten, and for the ice to melt and dilute the drink. For this reason, some hosts still use smaller glass sizes, preferring to mix a second drink at full strength and flavor.

Chilling and Frosting Glasses

Many bartenders make sure of cold cocktails by chilling the glasses beforehand. The simplest way to chill a glass is to place it in the refrigerator for 30 minutes, or in the freezer for 5 minutes (10 minutes if you want the glass to frost). If the refrigerator is full, or not handy to the bar, you can fill the glasses with ice cubes or cracked ice while you mix the drinks, discarding the ice when you are ready to pour.

To sugar-frost a glass for a Daiquiri, chill it first and then rub the inside and top of the rim with a strip of lime peel. Dip the moistened rim into a bowl of superfine sugar, pause a moment, lift the glass and tap it gently with a finger to shake off excess sugar. For the tequila-based Margarita cocktail, rub the chilled glass rim with lime peel and dip into salt.

Fruit Juices and Peels

Whenever possible, use fresh fruit for drinks that call for fruit flavoring. An orange, lemon or lime may be softened by rolling it on a hard surface, like a cutting board, bearing down with your hand. This helps to break down the fibers and makes it easier to extract the juice. In cutting lemon or lime peel, never include the white membrane of the rind; shave off only the colored surface peel, in sections about 1 inch by ½ inch for twisting.

Preparing Ice

Use only ice that has been isolated from foods in the refrigerator; if your refrigerator does not have a separate freezer chest, or if you store ice temporarily

WHISKEY SOUR (DELMONICO)	TOM COLLINS	WINE
5 to 7 ounces	10 to 14 ounces	8 to 10 ounces

near food, it may absorb undesirable odors. To rid ice of odors, rinse it quickly under cold water. Use ice cubes instead of shaved or cracked ice in shaker drinks to minimize dilution; if you have a temporary surplus of a cocktail left in a shaker or pitcher, remove the ice from the shaker to prevent diluting the drink while it waits.

To obtain the cracked ice certain recipes call for, use a manual or electric ice crusher, or a food blender equipped for this heavy-duty use. Or, simply wrap the cubes in a strong towel or double thickness of plastic wrap and break them up with a mallet or a hammer.

Gadgets

Of the many bar gadgets available in department stores and specialty shops, most perform useful functions, while others serve principally as decoration. The useful ones include a muddler, for crushing lump sugar and mixing it with bitters or other flavorings in the bottom of a glass; a waiter's corkscrew, with knife and cap opener; shot glasses, both for their literal use, to hold a "shot" of straight spirits, or for measuring ingredients for mixed drinks; a double-ended measure, doubly useful as its bowls are jigger-sized on one end, pony-sized on the other. Other serviceable items: a shaker and mixing glass set with a strainer, a martini or punch pitcher and a stirring rod, a lemon-lime squeezer, a long-handled bar spoon, measuring spoons and cup, an ice chipper, an ice shovel, a cutting board and knife, a blender, and a funnel.

Equivalents and Servings

1 dash = $1/16$ teaspoon	1 pint = 16 ounces = 8 to 10 servings
1 teaspoon = $1/8$ ounce	1 fifth = 25.6 ounces = 12 to 16 servings
1 tablespoon = $1/2$ ounce	1 quart = 32 ounces = 16 to 20 servings
1 pony = 1 ounce	1 bottle wine = 24 ounces = 6 servings
1 jigger = $1\frac{1}{2}$ ounces	1 split champagne = $6\frac{1}{2}$ ounces = 2 servings
8 ounces = 1 cup	1 quart champagne = 26 ounces = 6 to 8 servings
	1 magnum champagne = 52 ounces = 14 to 16 servings

Whiskey

Boston Ward 8
To make 1 cocktail

1 ounce fresh lemon juice
3 ounces bourbon
½ ounce grenadine
3 to 4 ice cubes
1 slice orange
A dash of cold club soda

An 8-ounce wine glass,
    chilled

Combine the lemon juice, bourbon, grenadine and ice cubes in a mixing glass. Place a shaker on top of the mixing glass and, grasping them firmly together, shake vigorously. Remove the shaker, place a strainer on top of the mixing glass, and pour into the chilled glass. Garnish with the slice of orange. Rinse the shaker with the dash of club soda and pour into the glass.

Horse's Neck
To make 1 tall drink

1 lemon
2 to 3 ice cubes
8 to 10 ounces cold ginger ale

A straw
A Tom Collins glass

With a small, sharp knife, peel a lemon in one continuous spiral so that it resembles a corkscrew. Place the peel in a Tom Collins glass, leaving just enough peel hanging over the edge of the glass so that it stays upright. Place 2 to 3 ice cubes in the glass, fill with ginger ale, and serve with a straw.

The original English or Irish Horse's Neck was a whiskey drink, and one variation still popular in the British Isles is made as above with the addition of 3 ounces of brandy and the substitution of 5 to 7 ounces of Irish ginger ale for the ginger ale. During Prohibition, the American version of the Horse's Neck lost its alcoholic content.

Manhattan
To make 1 cocktail

3/4 ounce sweet vermouth
2 1/2 ounces blended whiskey
A dash of Angostura bitters
2 to 3 ice cubes
1 maraschino cherry
1 strip orange peel

A 4-ounce cocktail glass, chilled

Combine the vermouth, whiskey, bitters and ice cubes in a mixing glass. With a bar spoon, stir gently, or you will "bruise" the spirits and cloud the drink. Place the cherry in the chilled cocktail glass, put a strainer on top of the mixing glass, and pour into the chilled glass. Twist the orange peel over the drink to release its oil, and rub the cut edge of the peel around the inner rim of the glass, but do not drop it in.

Dry Manhattan
To make 1 cocktail

1/2 ounce dry vermouth
3 ounces blended whiskey
3 to 4 ice cubes
1 strip lemon peel or a pitted green
   olive

A 4-ounce cocktail glass, chilled

Combine the vermouth, whiskey and ice cubes in a mixing glass and stir gently so as not to "bruise" the alcohol. Place a strainer over the mixing glass, pour into the chilled cocktail glass, and add the lemon peel (twisted to release the oil) or olive.

Perfect Manhattan
To make 1 cocktail

½ ounce sweet vermouth
½ ounce dry vermouth
2 ounces blended whiskey
3 to 4 ice cubes
1 strip orange or lemon peel

A 4-ounce cocktail glass, chilled

Combine the sweet and dry vermouths, the whiskey and the ice cubes in a mixing glass and stir together gently. Place a strainer over the top of the mixing glass and pour into the chilled cocktail glass. Twist the orange or lemon peel over the glass to release its oil, and add it to the drink.

Mint Julep
To make 1 tall drink

1½ teaspoons superfine or
    confectioners' sugar
6 to 8 sprigs fresh mint
A dash of cold water
1 to 1½ cups shaved ice
4 ounces bourbon
2 slices lemon
¼ teaspoon confectioners' sugar
2 to 3 drops brandy

A straw
An 8-ounce highball glass

Place 1½ teaspoons of sugar, 5 or 6 sprigs of the fresh mint and a dash of cold water in a highball glass. Use a muddler to crush the mint until it is well bruised and to dissolve the sugar. Fill the glass almost to the top with shaved ice, packing it down firmly. Pour in the bourbon and, with a long-handled bar spoon, use a chopping motion to mix it with the ice. Dry the outside of the glass with paper towels and place the glass in the refrigerator for at least an hour or in the freezer for about ½ hour. The glass should be thoroughly frosted and the ice inside almost solid.

Remove the glass from the freezer or refrigerator, touching the outside as little as possible with the bare hand so that it remains frosted; try to use paper towels or a napkin. Garnish the drink with the slices of lemon, "plant" the remaining 2 or 3 sprigs of mint in the ice, and sprinkle the mint with ¼ teaspoon sugar. Drop 2 or 3 drops of brandy on top and serve with a straw.

Mint juleps are frequently served in silver mugs, because these frost better than glass, or in glass mugs with handles; the handles keep the warm hand from touching the frosted surface. It is a good idea to serve large coasters or napkins with mint juleps, as the frost from the glasses or mugs melts and drips. Some recipes do not advise bruising the mint. The bruised-mint version given here results in a pronounced mint flavor, but if you do not care for this, do not crush the leaves.

Morning Glory
To make 1 cocktail

1½ ounces fresh lemon juice
1 teaspoon superfine sugar
2½ ounces Scotch
6 drops Pernod
1 egg white
2 teaspoons heavy cream
3 to 4 ice cubes

A 6-ounce cocktail glass, chilled

Combine the lemon juice and sugar in a mixing glass and stir with a bar spoon to dissolve the sugar. Add the Scotch, Pernod, egg white, heavy cream and ice cubes. Place a shaker on top of the mixing glass and, grasping them firmly together with both hands, shake vigorously 6 or 7 times. Remove the shaker, place a strainer on top of the mixing glass, and pour into the cocktail glass.

Old-fashioned
To make 1 cocktail

½ lump sugar
A dash of Angostura bitters
A drop of cold water
2 to 3 ice cubes
3 ounces bourbon, Scotch or blended
    whiskey
1 strip lemon peel
1 slice orange (optional)
1 maraschino cherry (optional)

An old-fashioned glass

In an old-fashioned glass, place the ½ lump of sugar, dash of bitters and drop of cold water. With a muddler, crush the sugar so that it is completely dissolved: if it is not, it will cloud the drink. Add the ice cubes and whiskey and stir well. Twist the lemon peel over the drink, releasing the oil, twirl the cut edge of the peel around the inside rim of the glass, and drop it in.

Sometimes a slice of orange and/or a maraschino cherry are added.

Presbyterian
To make 1 highball

2 to 3 ice cubes
3 ounces bourbon
2 ounces cold ginger ale
2 ounces cold club soda
1 strip lemon peel

An 8-ounce highball glass

Combine the ice cubes, bourbon, ginger ale and club soda in a highball glass and stir. Twist the lemon peel over the glass to release its oil, and drop it in.

Rob Roy
To make 1 cocktail

½ ounce sweet vermouth
3 ounces Scotch
6 to 8 ice cubes
1 strip orange peel

A 4-ounce cocktail glass

Combine the vermouth and Scotch in a mixing glass and fill with ice cubes. Stir gently, to chill and dilute the drink, then place a strainer on top of the mixing glass and pour into the cocktail glass. Twist the orange peel over the glass to release the oil, twirl the cut edge of the peel around the inside rim of the glass, and add the peel to the drink.

To make a dry Rob Roy, use a light Scotch and change the proportion to 3½ ounces of Scotch and 1 teaspoon of dry vermouth.

Rusty Nail
To make 1 after-dinner drink

1½ ounces Scotch
1½ ounces Drambuie
2 ice cubes

An old-fashioned glass

Combine the Scotch and Drambuie in an old-fashioned glass, add the ice cubes, and stir gently.

Sazerac (or Zazarac)

To make 1 cocktail

3 ounces bourbon or blended whiskey
½ teaspoon superfine sugar
1 ice cube
1 strip lemon peel
5 drops Peychaud bitters
3 drops Ojen (Spanish absinthe) or
　　substitute Pernod

An old-fashioned glass

Place the whiskey and sugar in an old-fashioned glass and stir with a bar spoon to dissolve the sugar. Add the ice cube and lemon peel, and top with the bitters and absinthe or Pernod. Stir briefly.

Scotch Mist

To make 1 cocktail

3 ounces Scotch
2 strips lemon peel
4 ounces shaved ice

An old-fashioned glass, chilled

Place the Scotch in a mixing glass and twist the strips of lemon peel over the glass, releasing the oil. Drop them in and add the shaved ice. Place a shaker on top of the mixing glass and, grasping them firmly together with both hands, shake vigorously 6 or 7 times. Remove the shaker and pour the entire contents into the chilled glass.

Whiskey Highball
To make 1 highball

2 ounces whiskey
2 ice cubes
4 to 6 ounces cold club soda or ginger
     ale

A 6- to 8-ounce highball glass

A highball may be defined as a tall iced drink consisting of a generous jig-
ger (or more) of whiskey, ice cubes and enough carbonated beverage to
nearly fill the highball glass. Use a glass stirring rod to stir quickly and
lightly. It is advisable to make a medium highball of 6 to 8 ounces rather
than a taller one, because the ice melts and dilutes the drink as it stands.
   The most popular combinations for highballs are bourbon and club
soda, Scotch and club soda, and blended whiskey (also called rye) and ginger ale or club soda. Bourbon and Scotch are often preferred with cold
water instead of club soda.

Whiskey Sour
To make 1 cocktail

1 ounce fresh lemon juice
3 ounces blended whiskey
1 teaspoon superfine sugar
3 to 4 ice cubes
1 maraschino cherry
1 slice orange

A 4-ounce Delmonico or whiskey
     sour glass, chilled

Combine the lemon juice, whiskey and sugar in a mixing glass, and stir
with a bar spoon to dissolve the sugar. Add the ice cubes. Place a shaker
on top of the mixing glass and, grasping them firmly together with both
hands, shake vigorously. Place the cherry and the orange slice in the
chilled glass. Remove the shaker, place a strainer on top of the mixing
glass, and pour into the chilled glass.
   There are numerous variations of the whiskey sour, all made in precise-
ly the same way. Brandy, apricot brandy, Scotch, bourbon, applejack,
rum or gin may be substituted for the blended whiskey.

Gin

The Bronx
To make 1 cocktail

½ ounce sweet vermouth
½ ounce dry vermouth
2½ ounces gin
¼ orange
3 to 4 ice cubes

A 4-ounce cocktail glass, chilled

Combine the sweet and dry vermouths, gin, juice of ¼ orange and ice cubes in a mixing glass. Drop the squeezed orange quarter into the mixing glass, place a shaker on top and, grasping them firmly together with both hands, shake well. Remove the shaker, place a strainer on top of the mixing glass, and pour into the cocktail glass.

Dry Martini
To make 1 cocktail

¼ ounce dry vermouth
2½ ounces gin
3 to 4 ice cubes
1 strip lemon peel

A 4-ounce cocktail glass, chilled

The "original" Martini, introduced as the Martinez around 1860, started out as 1 part gin to 1 part dry vermouth. By 1890, when the name changed to Martini, the ratio was 2 parts gin to 1 part vermouth. The change in ratio has continued through the years, generally becoming 1 part drier each 30 years. The standard Martini today is about 4½ parts gin to 1 part dry vermouth. Some, however, prefer a ratio closer to 10 to 1.

No doubt every Martini drinker has a firm commitment to his or her own method. Some use only a dash of vermouth, others merely wave the vermouth cork over the glass. Because of the change in personal preferences in the past decade, dry vermouth and gin are drier than ever before. For this reason, they are believed by many experts to produce too raw a drink when simply stirred. Shaking quickly with ice not only blends the Martini and results in a smoother taste but also chills the drink quickly and thoroughly, obviating the need for the ice cubes that would dilute it.

Combine the dry vermouth, gin and ice cubes in a mixing glass. Place a shaker on top of the glass and, grasping them firmly together with both hands, shake quickly 5 or 6 times. Rub the cut edge of the lemon peel around the inside rim of a chilled cocktail glass. Remove the shaker, place a strainer over the mixing glass and pour the Martini into the cocktail glass. Add the lemon peel.

Variations include a pitted olive in place of the lemon peel; a Gibson, made similarly, but with only a dash of vermouth and the addition of a pearl onion; and a vodka Martini.

Perfect Martini
To make 1 cocktail

½ ounce sweet vermouth
½ ounce dry vermouth
1½ ounces gin
3 to 4 ice cubes
1 strip orange peel

A 4-ounce cocktail glass, chilled

Combine the sweet and dry vermouths and the gin in a mixing glass, add the ice cubes and stir with a bar spoon to blend and chill the liquors. Place a strainer on top of the mixing glass and pour into a chilled cocktail glass. Twist the orange peel over the cocktail glass to release the oil, run the cut edge of the peel around the inside rim of the glass, and drop it in.

Sweet Martini
To make 1 cocktail

2 ounces sweet vermouth
2 ounces gin
1 maraschino cherry
1 strip orange peel

A 4-ounce cocktail glass, chilled

Combine the sweet vermouth and gin in the chilled cocktail glass and stir briefly. Garnish with a cherry and orange peel.

In England, this drink is known as gin and it—"it" referring to Italian sweet vermouth.

Gimlet
To make 1 cocktail

3 ounces gin or vodka
2 ice cubes
2 ounces Rose's sweetened lime juice
1 slice lime

A 6-ounce wine or cocktail glass,
   chilled

Place the gin or vodka in a 6-ounce glass and add the ice cubes. Top with lime juice and garnish with a slice of lime.

You may, if you wish, substitute fresh lime juice for the bottled juice. In that case, add ½ teaspoon of sugar to the gin or vodka in the glass and stir with a bar spoon to dissolve.

Gin and Bitters (or Pink Gin)
To make 1 cocktail

A dash of Angostura bitters
3 ounces gin
1 ice cube (optional)

A 4-ounce cocktail glass, chilled

Dash 2 or 3 drops of bitters into the cocktail glass and swirl it all around the bottom and sides of the glass. Then shake it out. Pour in the gin and, if you wish, add the ice cube.

Gin and Tonic
To make 1 tall drink

2 ice cubes
3 ounces gin
4 to 6 ounces cold quinine water
1 slice lemon or lime

A highball glass

Place the ice cubes in a highball glass and add the gin. Fill the glass with quinine water and garnish with a slice of lemon or lime. Do not stir.

In recent years, vodka and tonic has become a popular variation.

Gin Fizz
To make 1 tall drink

1½ ounces fresh lemon juice
3 ounces gin
1 teaspoon superfine sugar
3 to 4 ice cubes
2 ounces cold club soda

An 8-ounce highball glass, chilled

Place the lemon juice, gin and sugar in a mixing glass and stir with a bar spoon to dissolve the sugar. Add the ice cubes and place a shaker on top of the mixing glass. Grasping them firmly together with both hands, shake vigorously 8 to 10 times. Remove the shaker, place a strainer over the mixing glass, and pour into the chilled highball glass. Rinse the shaker with the club soda and pour into the glass.

A sloe gin fizz is made the same way, substituting sloe gin (not a gin but a liqueur made from blackthorn berries) for the dry gin and using only ½ teaspoon of sugar.

Gin Rickey
To make 1 tall drink

2 ice cubes
Juice of ½ lime
3 ounces gin
4 ounces cold club soda

A highball glass

Place the ice cubes in the highball glass and add the juice of ½ lime and the gin. Fill the glass with cold club soda and stir briefly.

Variations of the gin rickey can be made with applejack, bourbon, brandy, rum, blended whiskey, Scotch or sloe gin. When made with water instead of soda, the drink is called a gin sling.

Golden Fizz
To make 1 cocktail

1½ ounces fresh lemon juice
3 ounces gin
1 teaspoon superfine sugar
1 whole egg
3 to 4 ice cubes
2 ounces cold club soda

An 8-ounce wine or cocktail
    glass, chilled

Combine the lemon juice, gin and sugar in a mixing glass and stir with a bar spoon to dissolve the sugar. Add the whole egg and ice cubes. Place a shaker on top of the mixing glass and, grasping them firmly together with both hands, shake vigorously 6 or 7 times. Remove the shaker, place a strainer on top of the mixing glass, and pour into the chilled wine or cocktail glass. Rinse the shaker with the cold club soda and pour into the glass.

Magnolia
To make 1 cocktail

1 egg white
Juice of 1 lemon
3 ounces gin
$^{1}/_{2}$ teaspoon grenadine
A dash of heavy cream
3 to 4 ice cubes

An 8-ounce wine glass, chilled

Combine the egg white, lemon juice, gin, grenadine, heavy cream and ice in a mixing glass. Place a shaker on top of the mixing glass and, grasping them firmly together with both hands, shake vigorously 8 to 10 times. Remove the shaker, place a strainer on top, and pour into the chilled glass.

Silver Fizz
To make 1 cocktail

$1^{1}/_{2}$ ounces fresh lemon juice
3 ounces gin
1 teaspoon superfine sugar
1 egg white
A dash of heavy cream
3 to 4 ice cubes
2 ounces cold club soda

An 8-ounce wine or cocktail
   glass, chilled

Combine the lemon juice, gin and sugar in a mixing glass and stir with a bar spoon to dissolve the sugar. Add the egg white, dash of heavy cream and ice cubes. Place a shaker on top of the mixing glass and, grasping them firmly together with both hands, shake vigorously 6 or 7 times. Remove the shaker, place a strainer on top of the mixing glass, and pour into the chilled glass. Rinse the shaker with the cold club soda and pour into the drink.

To make a Ramos gin fizz, popular in New Orleans, follow the same instructions as above, but use 1 teaspoon of heavy cream and add 2 dashes of orange flower water.

Snowball Fizz
To make 1 cocktail

2 ounces fresh grapefruit juice
1 ounce fresh orange juice
1 teaspoon superfine sugar
3 ounces gin
1 egg white
3 to 4 ice cubes

An 8-ounce cocktail or wine
   glass, chilled

Combine the grapefruit and orange juice, sugar and gin in a mixing glass, and stir with a bar spoon to dissolve the sugar. Add the egg white and ice cubes. Place a shaker on top of the mixing glass and, grasping them firmly together with both hands, shake vigorously 8 or 10 times. Remove the shaker, place a strainer on top of the mixing glass, and pour into the cocktail or wine glass.

Negroni
To make 1 cocktail

2 ice cubes
1½ ounces Carpano or sweet
   vermouth
1½ ounces Campari bitters
1½ ounces gin
1 strip lemon peel

A 6-ounce old-fashioned glass

Place the ice cubes in the old-fashioned glass and add the Carpano or sweet vermouth, bitters and gin. Stir the ingredients together briefly and drop in the lemon peel.

Orange Blossom (or Golden Gate)
To make 1 cocktail

1½ ounces fresh orange juice
2½ ounces gin
Pinch of superfine sugar (optional)
3 to 4 ice cubes

A 4-ounce cocktail glass, chilled

Combine the orange juice, gin, sugar if you wish, and the ice cubes in a mixing glass. Place a shaker on top of the glass and, grasping them firmly together with both hands, shake well. Remove the shaker, place a strainer on top of the glass, and strain into a cocktail glass.
  When vodka is used instead of gin, the drink is called a screwdriver.

Pine Valley
To make 1 cocktail

Juice of 1 lime
3 ounces gin
2 to 3 sprigs fresh mint
½ egg white
½ teaspoon superfine sugar
3 to 4 ice cubes

A 6-ounce cocktail glass, chilled

Combine the juice of a lime, the gin, sprigs of mint, ½ egg white and sugar in a mixing glass and add the ice cubes. Place a shaker on top of the mixing glass and, grasping them firmly together with both hands, shake vigorously, making sure that the mint is well bruised. Remove the shaker, place a strainer on top of the mixing glass, and pour into the cocktail glass.

Pink Lady (or Clover Club)
To make 1 cocktail

½ ounce fresh lemon juice
2½ ounces gin
1 teaspoon grenadine
1 egg white
A dash of heavy cream
3 to 4 ice cubes

A 4-ounce cocktail glass, chilled

Combine the lemon juice, gin, grenadine, egg white, cream and ice cubes in a mixing glass. Place a shaker on top of the mixing glass and, grasping them firmly together with both hands, shake vigorously 10 or 12 times. Remove the shaker, place a strainer on top, and pour into a chilled cocktail glass.

Rose Cocktail (or French Manhattan)
To make 1 cocktail

2 dashes Fiel's orange bitters
½ ounce sweet vermouth
½ ounce dry vermouth
½ ounce cherry brandy
½ ounce kirsch
1 ounce gin
1 strip orange peel
1 maraschino cherry

A 4-ounce cocktail glass, chilled

Combine the orange bitters, 2 vermouths, cherry brandy, kirsch and gin in a 4-ounce cocktail glass and stir very gently so as not to cloud it. Twist the orange peel over the glass to release the oil and add the peel and the cherry to the cocktail.

Singapore Sling

To make 1 tall drink

2 ice cubes, whole or cracked
½ ounce Cherry Heering, or
 substitute cherry brandy
½ ounce fresh lemon juice
3 ounces gin
2 to 4 ounces cold water

An 8-ounce highball glass

Combine the ice, Cherry Heering or brandy, lemon juice and gin in a highball glass. Fill the glass with cold water and stir.

The Singapore sling is said to have originated in the Raffles Hotel in Singapore, and some claim that the original drink had, in addition to the above ingredients, a few drops of Benedictine and brandy, a slice of orange and a sprig of fresh mint. Many recipes substitute club soda for the cold water; although tasty, this would then be called a Singapore rickey and not a Singapore sling.

Tom Collins

To make 1 tall drink

1 ounce fresh lemon juice
3 ounces gin
1½ teaspoons superfine sugar
2 ice cubes
6 ounces cold club soda
1 slice orange (optional)
1 maraschino cherry (optional)

A Tom Collins glass

Place the lemon juice, gin and sugar in the Tom Collins glass and stir with a bar spoon to dissolve the sugar. Add the ice cubes, fill the glass with cold soda, and stir briefly. Garnish the drink, if you like, with an orange slice and/or a cherry.

Rum is the liquor most frequently substituted for gin—and the drink is then called a rum Collins—but applejack, bourbon, brandy, blended whiskey, Scotch or vodka can be also substituted. With bourbon or blended whiskey, the drink is called a John Collins.

White Lady
To make 1 cocktail

½ ounce fresh lemon juice
2½ ounces gin
1 ounce Cointreau or Triple Sec
3 to 4 ice cubes

A 4-ounce cocktail glass, chilled

Combine the lemon juice, gin and Cointreau or Triple Sec in a mixing glass and add the ice cubes. Place a shaker on top of the mixing glass and, grasping them firmly together with both hands, shake vigorously. Remove the shaker, place a strainer on top of the glass, and pour into a cocktail glass.

Vodka

Black Russian

To make 1 cocktail or after-dinner
    drink

1 ounce Kahlúa (coffee liqueur)
3 ounces vodka
2 to 3 ice cubes

A 4-ounce cocktail glass, chilled

Combine the Kahlúa and vodka in a mixing glass, add the ice cubes, and stir gently to combine. Place a strainer over the mixing glass and pour into the chilled cocktail glass.

Bloody Mary

To make 1 cocktail

8 to 12 ice cubes
2 teaspoons fresh lemon juice
4 ounces full-bodied tomato juice
3 ounces vodka
2 drops Worcestershire sauce
2 drops Tabasco
Freshly ground black pepper
A dash of celery salt (optional)

An 8-ounce wine glass

Fill a mixing glass with ice cubes and add the lemon juice, tomato juice, vodka, Worcestershire sauce and Tabasco. Season with a few grindings of black pepper. Place a shaker on top of the mixing glass and, grasping them firmly together with both hands, shake vigorously. Remove the shaker, place a strainer on top of the mixing glass, and strain into the wine glass. Sprinkle the top with a dash of celery salt if you wish.

    To serve the Bloody Mary "on the rocks," prepare as directed above and strain into an 8-ounce highball glass filled with 2 or 3 ice cubes.

    Recently a variation called a Danish Mary has become popular, substituting aquavit for vodka.

Bullshot
To make 1 cocktail

3 to 4 ice cubes
3 ounces vodka
4 ounces strong, cold beef bouillon
Salt
Freshly ground pepper

An 8-ounce wine glass, chilled

Combine the ice, vodka and beef bouillon in a mixing glass, add salt and pepper to taste, and stir with a bar spoon. Place a strainer on top of the mixing glass and pour into a chilled wine glass.

Moscow Mule
To make 1 tall drink

2 to 3 ice cubes
A dash of fresh lime juice
3 ounces vodka
4 to 6 ounces cold ginger beer
1 slice lime

A beer mug or 8-ounce glass

Place the ice cubes in a beer mug or heavy glass and add the lime juice and vodka. Fill the mug or glass with ginger beer and top with the slice of lime.

Salty Dog
To make 1 cocktail

3 ounces fresh grapefruit juice
4 ounces vodka
Pinch of superfine or confectioners'
    sugar
4 to 6 ice cubes

An 8-ounce wine glass, chilled

Combine the grapefruit juice, vodka, sugar and 4 or 5 ice cubes in a mixing glass, and stir gently with a bar spoon to dissolve the sugar and combine the ingredients. Place a strainer on top of the mixing glass and pour into the chilled wine glass. Add 1 ice cube to the wine glass if desired.

Sputnik
To make 1 pick-me-up

1 ounce Fernet-Branca
2 ounces vodka
½ teaspoon superfine sugar
1 teaspoon fresh lime or lemon juice
3 to 4 ice cubes

A 4-ounce cocktail glass, chilled

Combine the Fernet-Branca, vodka and sugar in a mixing glass and stir with a bar spoon to dissolve the sugar. Add the juice and ice cubes. Place a shaker on top of the mixing glass and, grasping them firmly together with both hands, shake vigorously 8 or 10 times. Remove the shaker, place a strainer over the mixing glass, and pour into a chilled cocktail glass.

Volga Boatman
To make 1 cocktail

Juice of ½ orange
3 ounces vodka
1 teaspoon kirsch
3 to 4 ice cubes

A 4-ounce cocktail glass, chilled

Combine the orange juice, vodka and kirsch in a mixing glass and add the ice cubes. Place a shaker on top of the glass and, grasping them firmly together with both hands, shake vigorously. Remove the shaker, place a strainer on top of the mixing glass, and pour into the cocktail glass.

White Russian (or Russian Bear)

To make 1 cocktail or after-dinner
  drink

1 ounce crème de cacao
2 ounces vodka
2 teaspoons heavy cream
3 to 4 ice cubes

A 4-ounce cocktail glass, chilled

Combine the crème de cacao, vodka, heavy cream and ice cubes in a mixing glass. Place a shaker on top of the glass and, grasping them firmly together with both hands, shake vigorously 6 or 7 times. Remove the shaker, place a strainer on top of the mixing glass, and pour into the chilled cocktail glass.

White Spider

To make 1 cocktail or after-dinner
  drink

2 ounces vodka
1 ounce white crème de menthe
2 to 3 ice cubes

A 4-ounce cocktail glass, chilled

Combine the vodka, white crème de menthe and ice cubes in a mixing glass and stir gently with a bar spoon to combine and chill the ingredients. Place a strainer on top of the mixing glass and pour into the cocktail glass.

A variation of the White Spider is called the Green Dragon—made with green crème de menthe instead of white.

Zeus Cocktail

To make 1 cocktail

2 ounces Campari bitters
1 ounce vodka
2 ice cubes
1 strip lemon peel

An old-fashioned glass

Combine the Campari, vodka and ice cubes in an old-fashioned glass and stir. Twist the lemon peel over the glass to release the oil, and drop it in.

Rum

Bacardi
To make 1 cocktail

1 teaspoon grenadine
3 ounces light Bacardi rum
1 ounce fresh lime juice
3 to 4 ice cubes

A 4-ounce cocktail glass, chilled

Combine the grenadine, rum, lime juice and ice cubes in a mixing glass. Place a shaker on top of the mixing glass and, grasping them firmly together with both hands, shake vigorously. Remove the shaker, place a strainer over the mixing glass, and pour into a cocktail glass.

Cuba Libre
To make 1 tall drink

Juice of ½ lime
3 ounces rum
3 to 4 ice cubes
6 ounces cola drink
1 slice lime

A Tom Collins glass

Combine the juice of half a lime, the rum and ice cubes in a tall Tom Collins glass. Fill the glass with cola, stir, and garnish with a slice of lime.

Daiquiri
To make 1 cocktail

¾ ounce fresh lime juice
1 teaspoon superfine sugar
1 teaspoon Cointreau or Triple Sec
3 ounces light rum
3 to 4 ice cubes
Egg white (optional)

A 4-ounce cocktail glass, chilled

Combine the lime juice and sugar in a mixing glass and stir with a bar spoon to dissolve the sugar. Now add the Cointreau or Triple Sec, rum and ice. Place a shaker on top of the mixing glass and, grasping them firmly together with both hands, shake vigorously. Remove the shaker, place a strainer on top of the mixing glass, and pour into a cocktail glass.

To make your Daiquiri even foamier, try adding just a dash of egg white to the mixing glass before shaking.

Frozen Daiquiri
To make 1 cocktail

2 ounces fresh lime juice
1 teaspoon superfine sugar
1 teaspoon Cointreau or Triple Sec
3 ounces light rum
6 ounces shaved or cracked ice

A short straw
An 8-ounce wine glass, chilled

Combine the lime juice, sugar, Cointreau or Triple Sec, rum and ice in an electric blender, and blend for 20 seconds at medium speed. Pour the contents of the container, unstrained, into a large wine glass, and serve with a short straw.

Derby Daiquiri

To make 1 cocktail

½ ounce fresh lime juice
1 ounce fresh orange juice
1 teaspoon superfine sugar
1½ ounces light rum
1 cup shaved or finely cracked ice

A short straw
An 8-ounce wine glass, chilled

Combine the lime and orange juices, sugar, rum and ice in the container of an electric blender, and blend at medium speed for 20 seconds. Pour the contents of the container, unstrained, into the chilled glass and serve with a short straw.

Peach Daiquiri

To make 1 cocktail

½ fresh peach, peeled, or substitute
     ½ canned peach or 3 ounces frozen
     peaches
½ ounce fresh lime juice
1½ teaspoons superfine sugar
1½ ounces light rum
4 to 6 ounces shaved or finely cracked
     ice

An 8-ounce wine glass, chilled

Combine the peach, lime juice, sugar, rum and ice in the container of an electric blender, and blend at medium speed for 20 seconds. Pour the contents of the container, unstrained, into a large wine glass.

NOTE: If you have substituted a canned or frozen peach that has been packed in syrup, do not add any sugar.

El Presidente
To make 1 cocktail

½ ounce sweet vermouth
3 ounces light Bacardi rum
A dash of Angostura bitters
3 to 4 ice cubes
1 strip orange peel

A 4-ounce cocktail glass, chilled

Combine the sweet vermouth, rum, bitters and ice cubes in a mixing glass. Stir with a bar spoon, then place a strainer over the top of the mixing glass and pour into a chilled cocktail glass. Twist the orange peel over the glass to release the oil, and twirl it around the inside edge of the glass. Do not add it to the drink.

Mai-Tai
To make 1 cocktail

Juice of ½ lime
½ ounce apricot brandy
½ ounce curaçao
2 ounces dark Jamaica rum
3 to 4 ice cubes
1 stick fresh pineapple, about ½ inch
    wide and 2 to 3 inches long

A 4-ounce cocktail glass, chilled

Combine the juice of half a lime, the apricot brandy, curaçao, rum and ice cubes in a mixing glass. Place a shaker on top of the mixing glass and, grasping them together firmly with both hands, shake vigorously. Remove the shaker, place a strainer on top of the mixing glass, and pour into a cocktail glass. Garnish with a stick of fresh pineapple.

Planter's Punch
To make 1 tall drink

1½ ounces fresh lime juice
1 teaspoon brown sugar
4 ounces Jamaica rum
1½ to 2 cups finely shaved ice
2 slices lime
1 maraschino cherry
1 sprig fresh mint (optional)

A straw
A Tom Collins glass

Combine the lime juice and brown sugar in a Tom Collins glass. Stir with a muddler or bar spoon to dissolve the sugar, then add the rum. Fill the glass ¾ way with shaved ice and stir again. Decorate with the slices of lime and a cherry, and if you wish, the fresh mint. Serve with a straw.

Brandies and Liqueurs

Angel's Dream (or Alfonso)
To make 1 after-dinner drink

1½ ounces crème de cacao
3 dashes of heavy cream

A 2-ounce liqueur glass

Pour the crème de cacao into a liqueur glass. Drop the dashes of heavy cream into a small demitasse spoon and place the spoon in the glass on top of the liqueur. Let the cream slide off slowly—it must not mix with the liqueur but should float on the surface.

A variation of this drink is the Angel's Kiss, made by preparing the drink as above and then piercing a maraschino cherry with a toothpick and laying the toothpick across the top of the glass.

Between the Sheets
To make 1 after-dinner drink

½ ounce fresh lemon juice
1 ounce brandy
1 ounce Cointreau
1 ounce light rum
3 to 4 ice cubes

A 4-ounce cocktail glass, chilled

Combine the lemon juice, brandy, Cointreau, rum and ice cubes in a mixing glass. Place a shaker on top of the mixing glass and, grasping them firmly together with both hands, shake vigorously. Remove the shaker, place a strainer on top of the mixing glass, and pour into a chilled cocktail glass.

Brandy Alexander
To make 1 cocktail

1 ounce crème de cacao
2 ounces brandy
½ ounce (1 tablespoon) heavy cream
3 to 4 ice cubes

A 4-ounce cocktail glass, chilled

Combine the crème de cacao, brandy, heavy cream and ice cubes in a mixing glass. Set the shaker on top of the mixing glass and, grasping them firmly together with both hands, shake vigorously 7 or 8 times. Remove the shaker, place a strainer over the mixing glass, and pour into a cocktail glass.

A variation of this drink, called an Alexander, is made by substituting gin or vodka for the brandy.

Brandy Blazer
To make 1 after-dinner drink

1 lump sugar
1 strip lemon peel
1 strip orange peel
3½ ounces warmed brandy

A 4-ounce old-fashioned glass,
   warmed

Combine the sugar, lemon peel, orange peel and brandy in a warmed old-fashioned glass. Mash with a muddler to thoroughly dissolve the sugar, then ignite the brandy with a match.

Brandy Cocktail
To make 1 cocktail

½ teaspoon superfine sugar
3 drops Fiel's orange bitters
    (optional)
3 ounces brandy
3 to 4 ice cubes
3 strips orange peel

A 4-ounce cocktail glass, chilled

Place the sugar, orange bitters and brandy in a mixing glass, and stir with a bar spoon to dissolve the sugar. Add ice cubes; twist the orange peels over the glass to release their oil, then drop them in it. Place a shaker on top of the mixing glass and, grasping them firmly together with both hands, shake vigorously 7 or 8 times. Remove the shaker, place a strainer on top of the glass, and pour into a chilled cocktail glass.

Brandy Float
To make 1 after-dinner drink

4 ounces (½ cup) shaved or finely
    cracked ice
1½ ounces white crème de menthe
½ ounce brandy

A short straw
A 4-ounce cocktail glass

Fill a cocktail glass with shaved or finely cracked ice. Pour in the white crème de menthe. Pour the brandy on top of the crème de menthe very slowly, so that it floats on the surface. Serve with a short straw.

Brandy Milk Punch
To make 1 serving

1½ teaspoons superfine sugar
3 ounces brandy
5 ounces cold milk
3 to 4 ice cubes
Ground nutmeg

A highball or Tom Collins glass

Combine the sugar and brandy in a mixing glass and stir with a bar spoon to dissolve the sugar. Add the milk and ice. Place a shaker on top of the mixing glass and, grasping them firmly together with both hands, shake vigorously. Remove the shaker, place a strainer on top of the mixing glass, and pour into a tall glass. Sprinkle the top of the milk punch with ground nutmeg.

Variations of this drink can also be made with rum, bourbon, blended whiskey or Scotch.

Grasshopper
To make 1 after-dinner drink

1½ ounces crème de cacao
2½ ounces green crème de
    menthe
½ ounce (1 tablespoon) heavy cream
3 to 4 ice cubes

A 4-ounce cocktail glass, chilled

Combine the crème de cacao, green crème de menthe, heavy cream and ice cubes in a mixing glass. Place a shaker over the top of the mixing glass and, grasping them firmly together with both hands, shake vigorously 7 or 8 times. Remove the shaker, place a strainer on top of the mixing glass, and pour into a chilled cocktail glass.

Jack Rose
To make 1 cocktail

1 ounce fresh lemon juice
3 ounces applejack
½ teaspoon grenadine
3 to 4 ice cubes

A 4-ounce cocktail glass, chilled

In a mixing glass, combine the juice, applejack, grenadine and the ice cubes. Place a shaker on top of the mixing glass and, grasping them firmly together with both hands, shake vigorously 7 or 8 times. Remove the shaker, place a strainer over the mixing glass, and pour into a chilled cocktail glass.

Pernod Frappé
To make 1 cocktail

1 egg white
1½ teaspoons superfine sugar
A dash of heavy cream
4 ounces Pernod
3 to 4 ice cubes

A 6-ounce wine glass, chilled

Combine the egg white and sugar in a mixing glass, and stir with a bar spoon to dissolve the sugar. Add the heavy cream, Pernod and ice cubes. Place a shaker on top of the mixing glass and, grasping them firmly together with both hands, shake vigorously 8 or 10 times. Remove the shaker, place a strainer on top of the glass, and pour into a wine glass.

Margarita I
To make 1 cocktail

1 slice lemon
Coarse (kosher) salt
½ ounce fresh lemon juice
1½ teaspoons superfine sugar
2 ounces tequila
3 to 4 ice cubes

A 4-ounce cocktail glass, chilled

Rub the inside rim of the chilled cocktail glass with the slice of lemon. Pour salt into a saucer or cup and dip in the glass so that a thin layer of salt adheres to the moistened rim of the glass.

Combine the lemon juice and sugar in a mixing glass and stir with a muddler or bar spoon to dissolve the sugar. Add the tequila and ice cubes and place a shaker on top of the mixing glass. Grasping them firmly together with both hands, shake vigorously 6 or 7 times. Remove the shaker, place a strainer on top of the mixing glass, and pour into the salt-rimmed cocktail glass.

Margarita II
To make 1 cocktail

1 slice lime
Coarse (kosher) salt
½ ounce fresh lime juice
1½ ounces tequila
½ ounce Triple Sec
3 to 4 ice cubes

A 4-ounce cocktail glass, chilled

Rub the inside rim of the chilled cocktail glass with the slice of lime. Pour salt into a saucer or cup and dip in the glass so that a thin layer of salt adheres to the moistened rim of the glass.

Combine the lime juice, tequila, Triple Sec and ice cubes in a mixing glass and place a shaker on top. Grasping them firmly together with both hands, shake vigorously 6 or 7 times. Remove the shaker, place a strainer on top of the mixing glass, and pour into the salt-rimmed cocktail glass.

Pousse-Café
To make 1 after-dinner drink

VARIATION I
¼ ounce (1½ teaspoons) green crème
   de menthe
¼ ounce (1½ teaspoons) yellow
   Chartreuse
¼ ounce (1½ teaspoons) Cherry
   Heering
¼ ounce (1½ teaspoons) cognac

VARIATION II
¼ ounce crème d'amande
¼ ounce white crème de menthe
¼ ounce Grand Marnier

VARIATION III
½ ounce parfait amour
½ ounce Crème Yvette

A 1- to 2-ounce cordial or liqueur
   glass

A pousse-café, often called a rainbow cordial, is an after-dinner drink composed of differently colored liqueurs poured into a tall, narrow cordial glass one at a time so that the ingredients remain separate and do not combine. Two to seven liqueurs can be used, but you must start with the heaviest so that the layers will remain in individual suspension. A steady hand—and considerable patience—is required to make this showy, spectacular drink successfully. Unfortunately, it is impossible to chart the weights of the various liqueurs since a flavor may vary in density from one distiller to another. Trial and error may be necessary until you find the combination of weights, colors and flavors that suits you.

Place the liqueur glass on a flat, steady surface and pour in the green crème de menthe. Place a demitasse spoon upside down in the glass and very slowly pour the yellow Chartreuse over the back of the spoon, letting it trickle off onto the crème de menthe. Complete this layer of liqueur, wipe the spoon dry, and proceed with the Cherry Heering. As the cognac is very light, it will float on top.

   Two other combinations have been suggested in the ingredients list and should be poured in the order given.

Pimm's Cup No. 1
To make 1 tall drink

Juice of 1 lime
1 teaspoon superfine sugar
2 to 3 ice cubes
3 ounces Pimm's No. 1
1 lemon slice
2 strips cucumber peel
4 to 6 ounces cold club or lemon
    soda
1 sprig fresh mint (optional)

A Tom Collins glass

Combine the lime juice and sugar in a Tom Collins glass and stir with a
bar spoon to dissolve the sugar. Add the ice cubes, Pimm's No. 1 (a gin-
based liqueur) and the slice of lemon. With a vegetable peeler or small,
sharp knife, cut 2 peels lengthwise from a cucumber and stand the cucumber peels upright in the glass. Fill with club or lemon soda and
garnish, if you like, with a sprig of fresh mint.

Red Lion
To make 1 cocktail

2 to 3 drops Fiel's orange bitters
    (optional)
½ ounce fresh lemon juice
½ ounce fresh orange juice
2 ounces Grand Marnier
1 ounce gin
1 strip orange peel
3 to 4 ice cubes

A 4-ounce cocktail glass, chilled

Combine the bitters, lemon and orange juices, Grand Marnier and gin in
a mixing glass. Twist the orange peel over the glass to release the oil and
then drop it in. Add ice cubes, and place a shaker on top of the mixing
glass. Grasping them firmly together with both hands, shake vigorously 6
or 7 times. Remove the shaker, place a strainer on top of the mixing
glass, and pour into the cocktail glass.

Sidecar

To make 1 cocktail or after-dinner
   drink

1 ounce Cointreau or Triple Sec
2 ounces brandy
½ ounce fresh lemon juice
3 to 4 ice cubes

A 4-ounce cocktail glass, chilled

Combine the Cointreau or Triple Sec, brandy, lemon juice and ice cubes
in a mixing glass. Place a shaker on top of the mixing glass and, grasping
them firmly together with both hands, shake vigorously 7 or 8 times. Remove the shaker, place a strainer on top of the mixing glass, and pour
into a chilled cocktail glass.

Stinger

To make 1 after-dinner drink

3 ounces brandy
1 ounce white crème de menthe
3 to 4 ice cubes

A 4-ounce cocktail glass, chilled

Combine the brandy, white crème de menthe and ice cubes in a mixing
glass. Place a shaker on top of the mixing glass and, grasping them firmly together with both hands, shake vigorously 6 or 7 times. Remove the
shaker, place a strainer over the mixing glass, and pour into a chilled cocktail glass.

Suissesse

To make 1 cocktail

1 egg white
1½ ounces anisette
3 ounces Pernod
A dash of heavy cream
3 to 4 ice cubes

A 4- to 6-ounce cocktail glass, chilled

Combine the egg white, anisette, Pernod, cream and ice cubes in a mixing glass. Place a shaker on top of the glass and, grasping them firmly together with both hands, shake vigorously 8 or 10 times. Remove the shaker, place a strainer on top of the mixing glass, and pour into a cocktail glass.

Tomate

To make 1 tall drink

2 ice cubes
4 ounces Pernod
1½ teaspoons grenadine
Cold water

An 8-ounce wine glass

Place the 2 ice cubes in a large wine glass and pour in the Pernod and grenadine. Fill the glass with 2 to 3 ounces of cold water and stir.

Wines

Americano
To make 1 apéritif

4 ounces Carpano or sweet vermouth
1½ ounces Campari bitters
1 strip orange peel
2 ice cubes
2 ounces cold club soda

An 8-ounce wine glass

Place the Carpano or sweet vermouth and bitters in an 8-ounce wine glass. Twist the orange peel over the glass to release the oil, rub the cut edge of the peel around the inside of the rim, and drop the peel into the glass. Add the ice cubes, fill with club soda, and stir.

Black Velvet
To make 1 tall drink

6 ounces cold Guinness stout
6 ounces (1 split) cold champagne

A Tom Collins glass, chilled

The traditional way of making a Black Velvet is to hold the cold stout in one hand, the cold champagne in the other, and to pour them into the tall, cold glass simultaneously. A simpler way is to pour in the stout first, and then very slowly fill the glass with champagne. Do not stir, but drink immediately, before the bubbles die and the taste flattens.

Champagne Cocktail
To make 1 cocktail

6 ounces cold champagne
1 strip orange peel
1 teaspoon brandy

A 6- to 8-ounce champagne glass,
    chilled

Pour the cold champagne into the glass, twist the orange peel over it to release the oil, and drop the peel in. Pour the brandy in slowly so that it
floats on the champagne.

Champagne Pick-Me-Up
To make 1 pick-me-up

1 ounce fresh orange juice
½ ounce fresh lemon juice
1 teaspoon grenadine
2 ounces brandy
3 to 4 ice cubes
4 ounces cold champagne

An 8-ounce wine glass, chilled

Combine the orange and lemon juices, grenadine, brandy and ice cubes
in a mixing glass. Place a shaker on top of the mixing glass and, grasping them firmly together with both hands, shake vigorously. Remove the
shaker, place a strainer on top of the mixing glass, and pour into a large
wine glass. Rinse the shaker with champagne and pour it slowly into the
wine glass.

Claret Lemonade
To make 1 tall drink

Juice of 1 lemon
1½ teaspoons superfine sugar
6 ounces cracked ice
8 to 10 ounces cold claret (Bordeaux)
2 slices of lemon

A straw
A Tom Collins glass

44

Place the lemon juice and sugar in a tall Tom Collins glass and stir with a bar spoon to dissolve the sugar thoroughly. Fill the glass halfway with the cracked ice, and fill with the claret. Garnish with slices of lemon and serve with a straw.

Dubonnet Cocktail
To make 1 cocktail

2 ounces red Dubonnet
1 ounce gin
A dash of Fiel's orange bitters
   (optional)
3 to 4 ice cubes
1 strip orange peel

A 4-ounce cocktail glass, chilled

Combine the Dubonnet, gin, orange bitters if you wish, and ice cubes in a mixing glass. Stir very gently with a bar spoon, place a strainer over the mixing glass, and pour into a cocktail glass. Twist the orange peel over the cocktail glass to release the oil, and rub the cut edge of the peel around the inside rim of the glass, but do not drop it in.

Kir
To make 1 cocktail

2 ice cubes
6 ounces dry white wine
½ ounce (1 tablespoon) crème de
   cassis
1 strip lemon peel

An 8-ounce wine glass

In a large wine glass combine the ice cubes, white wine and crème de cassis. Twist the lemon peel over the glass to release the oil, and drop the peel in. Stir gently.

French 75

To make 1 cocktail

1½ ounces fresh lemon juice
3 ounces gin
1 egg white
½ ounce (1 tablespoon) heavy cream
1½ teaspoons superfine sugar
3 to 4 ice cubes
3 ounces cold champagne

An 8-ounce wine or champagne glass,
    chilled

Combine the lemon juice, gin, egg white, cream, sugar and ice cubes in a mixing glass. Place a shaker on top of the glass and, grasping them firmly together with both hands, shake vigorously 10 to 12 times. Remove the shaker, place a strainer on top of the mixing glass, and pour into a chilled wine glass. Rinse the shaker with the champagne and pour into the glass.

Merry Widow

To make 1 apéritif

1½ ounces sherry
1½ ounces sweet vermouth
1 strip lemon peel
3 to 4 ice cubes

A 4-ounce cocktail or old-fashioned
    glass, chilled

Combine the sherry and vermouth in a mixing glass. Twist the lemon peel over the glass to release the oil, and drop the peel in. Add the ice cubes, stir gently with a bar spoon, and strain into a glass.

To make a variation known as the Duplex, substitute 1½ ounces of dry vermouth for the sherry.

Prairie Oyster

To make 1 pick-me-up

1 egg yolk
Freshly ground black pepper
1 tablespoon Worcestershire sauce
1½ ounces port
Celery salt

A 4-ounce wine or cocktail glass

Slide the egg yolk gently into the wine or cocktail glass, so that the yolk remains intact. Season it lightly with a few grindings of black pepper, add the Worcestershire sauce and float the port on the top. Sprinkle with celery salt and swallow the drink without breaking the yolk.

Sherry Flip

To make 1 cocktail

1 whole egg
1 teaspoon superfine sugar
3 ounces medium sherry
3 to 4 ice cubes
Ground nutmeg

A 6-ounce wine or whiskey sour glass,
    chilled

A flip—a drink in which a wine or spirit is briskly shaken with sugar and a whole egg—can be made with sherry, Madeira, Marsala, port, brandy, gin, light rum, vodka or whiskey.

Combine the egg, sugar, wine (or spirit) and ice cubes in a mixing glass. Place a shaker over the mixing glass and, grasping them firmly together with both hands, shake vigorously 10 or 12 times. Remove the shaker, place a strainer over the top of the mixing glass, and pour into a 6-ounce wine or whiskey sour glass. Sprinkle the top with nutmeg.

Coffee Cocktail

To make 1 cocktail

1 whole egg
2½ ounces medium sherry
1 teaspoon superfine sugar
1½ ounces brandy
3 to 4 ice cubes
Ground nutmeg

A 6-ounce wine or whiskey sour glass,
   chilled

Combine the egg, sherry, sugar, brandy and ice cubes in a mixing glass.
Place a shaker on top of the glass and, grasping them together firmly
with both hands, shake vigorously 7 or 8 times. Remove the shaker,
place a strainer on top of the mixing glass, and pour into a 6-ounce
glass. Sprinkle the top with a dash of nutmeg. (The coffee cocktail is simply a variation of the sherry flip.)

Spritzer

To make 1 tall drink

1 lemon
2 to 3 ice cubes
6 ounces cold Rhine wine, or
   substitute another dry white wine
4 ounces cold club soda

A Tom Collins glass

With a small, sharp knife, carefully peel the lemon in a spiral, as you
would an apple. The peel should be in 1 piece, resembling a corkscrew.
Drop the peel into the Tom Collins glass, add the ice cubes and white
wine, and fill the glass with cold club soda.

Vermouth Cassis
To make 1 apéritif

4 ounces dry vermouth
2 ice cubes
1 strip lemon peel
1½ teaspoons crème de cassis
2 ounces cold club soda

An 8-ounce wine glass

Pour the 4 ounces of dry vermouth into a large wine glass and add 2 ice cubes. Twist the lemon peel over the glass to release the oil, and drop the peel in. Add the crème de cassis, top with cold club soda, and stir gently.

Punches and Party Drinks

Champagne or Rhine Wine Cup
To serve 4

Approximately 1 cup of fruits of the
    season: peeled orange and/or
    grapefruit sections, lemon slices,
    hulled strawberries, peach slices,
    cucumber peel
4 maraschino cherries
4 ounces brandy
4 ounces Benedictine
4 ounces maraschino liqueur
12 to 16 ice cubes or a block of ice
1 bottle cold champagne or cold
    Rhine wine
6 ounces cold Perrier water or club
    soda

A 1½- to 2-quart pitcher or punch
    bowl
4 wine glasses or punch cups, chilled

The most crucial point in making this—and the following two—refreshing summer drinks is to be sure that the pitcher or bowl, glasses, wine, Perrier or club soda, and fruit are all thoroughly chilled.

Place the fruits of your choice in the pitcher first, then add the cherries and the brandy, Benedictine and maraschino liqueur. Place the pitcher or bowl in the refrigerator (or freezer) for at least 1 hour (½ hour if you use the freezer). Remove and fill with ice cubes. A solid block of ice that fits the pitcher or bowl is even better; it will be more attractive, and will not dilute the drink by melting too quickly.

Just before serving, pour in the champagne or Rhine wine and the sparkling water. Stir briefly with a glass stirring rod or a bar spoon and serve in chilled wine glasses or punch cups.

Claret Cup
To serve 4

Approximately 1 cup of fruits of the
    season: peeled orange and/or
    grapefruit sections, lemon slices,
    hulled strawberries, peach slices,
    cucumber peel
4 ounces blackberry brandy
4 ounces maraschino liqueur
4 ounces curaçao
12 to 16 ice cubes or a block of ice
1 bottle claret (Bordeaux)
6 ounces cold Perrier water or club
    soda

A 1½- to 2-quart pitcher or punch
    bowl
4 wine glasses or punch cups, chilled

Place the fruits of your choice in the pitcher or bowl first, then add the
blackberry brandy, maraschino liqueur and curaçao. Place the vessel in
the refrigerator (or freezer) for at least 1 hour (½ hour if you use the freezer). Remove and fill with ice cubes. A solid block of ice cut to fit the
pitcher or bowl is even better, since it will not melt as quickly and dilute
the drink. Pour in the claret and sparkling water, stir briefly, and serve in
chilled wine glasses or punch cups.

Sauternes Cup
To serve 4

Approximately 1 cup of fruits of the
   season: peeled orange and/or
   grapefruit sections, lemon slices,
   hulled strawberries, peach slices,
   cucumber peel
4 ounces brandy
4 ounces Cointreau
4 ounces Grand Marnier
12 to 16 ice cubes or a block of ice
1 bottle imported Sauternes
6 ounces cold Perrier water or club
   soda

A 1½- to 2-quart pitcher or punch
   bowl
4 wine glasses or punch cups, chilled

Place the fruits of your choice in the pitcher or bowl first, then add the brandy, Cointreau and Grand Marnier. Place the pitcher or bowl in the refrigerator (or freezer) for at least 1 hour (½ hour if you use the freezer). Remove and fill with ice cubes. A solid block of ice that fits the pitcher or bowl is even better, since it will not melt as quickly and dilute the drink. Pour in the Sauternes and sparkling water, stir briefly, and serve in chilled wine glasses or punch cups.

Sangría
To make 1 quart

½ cup superfine sugar
1 cup cold water
1 lime, thinly sliced
1 orange, thinly sliced
12 to 16 ice cubes
1 bottle red wine

A 1½- to 2-quart glass pitcher
4- to 6-ounce glasses, chilled

Combine the sugar and water in a small saucepan and place over moderate heat, stirring almost constantly with a wooden spoon until the sugar is dissolved. When the syrup just reaches the boiling point, remove the pan from the heat and add the thinly sliced lime and orange. Allow the fruit to marinate in the syrup for at least 4 hours at room temperature. Place the contents of an ice-cube tray in the glass pitcher and add 6 slices of the marinated fruit and ½ cup of the syrup. Fill the pitcher with the bottle of red wine. Place 1 slice of orange and 1 slice of lime in each glass and fill the glasses from the pitcher.

Fish House Punch
To make 1½ gallons

1½ cups superfine sugar
1 quart fresh lemon juice
2 quarts 100-proof Jamaica rum, or
    substitute 80-proof light or dark
    rum
2 quarts cold water
4 ounces peach brandy
1 quart cognac
A block of ice
1 cup sliced, peeled peaches, fresh,
    frozen or canned (optional)

A 2-gallon punch bowl
Punch cups

The original Fish House punch was made in the mid-18th Century at a fishing and social club called "State in Schuylkill" in Pennsylvania. The recipe called for 100-proof Jamaica rum, but as this results in a very heavy, somewhat smoky taste, contemporary American palates might prefer a lighter, 80-proof rum. Despite popular misconceptions, a true punch is made with plain water—fresh spring water if feasible —instead of any carbonated beverage.

Place the sugar and lemon juice in the punch bowl and stir with a muddler or bar spoon to dissolve the sugar thoroughly. Add the rum, water, peach brandy and cognac, stir to combine the ingredients, and allow the punch to "ripen" at room temperature for at least 2 hours, stirring occasionally. Put the solid block of ice in the bowl and garnish, if you like, with sliced peaches. Serve in punch cups.

Eggnog
To serve 1

1 whole egg
1½ teaspoons superfine sugar
1½ ounces Jamaica rum
2 ounces blended whiskey
4 ounces milk
3 to 4 ice cubes
Ground nutmeg
1 strip lemon peel

An 8- to 10-ounce highball or Tom
    Collins glass

Place the whole egg and sugar in a mixing glass and stir gently but thoroughly with a bar spoon to combine. Add the rum, whiskey and milk, and stir again. Now add the ice cubes, place a shaker on top of the mixing glass and, grasping them firmly together with both hands, shake vigorously 6 or 7 times. Remove the shaker, place a strainer on top of the mixing glass, and strain the eggnog into the highball glass. Sprinkle the top with nutmeg and twist the lemon peel over the top of the drink to release the oil; do not add it to the glass.

Holiday Eggnog
To serve 12

10 egg whites
⅓ cup superfine sugar
10 egg yolks
1 quart (2 pints) cold heavy cream
2 tablespoons superfine sugar
1 fifth (about 26 ounces) blended
   whiskey
12 ounces Jamaica rum
1 pint (2 cups) cold milk
Grated rind of 1 orange
Grated rind of 1 lemon
Ground nutmeg

A 2-gallon punch bowl
12 punch cups

Place the egg whites in a large mixing bowl and add the ⅓ cup of sugar. Beat the egg whites and sugar with a wire whisk or an electric or rotary beater until they thicken somewhat and foam. In another large bowl, beat the egg yolks until they thicken enough to drop back in the form of a ribbon when the beater is lifted out of the bowl. Pour the foamy egg whites and sugar into the beaten egg yolks and beat them together until they are thoroughly combined.

Place the cold heavy cream and 2 tablespoons of sugar in the punch bowl and beat until the cream doubles in volume and is thick enough to hold its shape softly. Now, beating constantly, slowly pour the egg mixture into the punch bowl with the whipped cream. When thoroughly combined, slowly add the whiskey and rum and then the cold milk, beating all the while. By this time, the eggnog will have thickened somewhat; it will thicken even more as it chills. Sprinkle the top of the eggnog with grated lemon and orange peel and the ground nutmeg and chill for at least 2 hours, or even overnight.

Hot Drinks

Café Brûlé (or Café Royale)
To make 1 after-dinner drink

3 strips lemon peel
A dish of superfine or confectioners'
   sugar
½ stick cinnamon
1½ ounces cognac
3 ounces hot coffee

An old-fashioned glass

Rub the cut edge of a strip of lemon peel around the inside rim of an old-fashioned glass and then dip the glass into the dish of sugar so that the sugar adheres to the inside rim. Twist the 2 other strips of peel over the glass to release their oil, and drop them and the ½ stick of cinnamon into the glass. Warm the cognac in a chafing dish or in a deep spoon held over a flame. Set a spoon in the glass to prevent the glass from cracking, pour in the warmed cognac, and set it aflame with a match. Let it burn itself out, then add the hot coffee and serve.

Café Brûlot
To serve 10 to 12

1 stick cinnamon
12 whole cloves
Peelings of 2 oranges, cut into thin
   slivers
Peelings of 2 lemons, cut into thin
   slivers
6 sugar lumps
8 ounces brandy
2 ounces curaçao
1 quart strong black coffee

About 1 dozen 8-ounce stemmed
   goblets, mugs or cups

This after-dinner drink, suitable for a party, was made famous by Brennan's Restaurant in New Orleans.

56

In a *brûlot* bowl or chafing dish, mash the cinnamon, cloves, orange peel, lemon peel and sugar lumps with a ladle. Add the brandy and curaçao and stir together. Carefully ignite the brandy, stepping back, since the flame might flare up, and mix until the sugar is dissolved. Gradually add the black coffee and continue mixing until the flame flickers out.

Grog
To make 1 hot drink

1 slice lemon
2 whole cloves
1 teaspoon superfine sugar
A 1-inch piece cinnamon stick
3 ounces Jamaica rum
4 ounces boiling water

An 8-ounce glass, preferably with
 handle

Stud the slice of lemon with the 2 cloves. Wash a glass with very hot water and shake it dry. Place the sugar, piece of cinnamon and slice of lemon in the warm glass, and add the rum. Stir with a spoon to dissolve the sugar, leave the spoon in the glass so that the glass will not crack, and fill with boiling water. Stir briefly and serve.

Glögg (Hot Mulled Wine)
To serve 20 to 25

2 quarts dry red wine
2 quarts muscatel
1 pint sweet vermouth
2 tablespoons Angostura bitters
2 cups raisins
Peelings of 1 orange
12 whole cardamoms, bruised in a
    mortar with a pestle or by covering
    with a towel and crushing with a
    rolling pin
10 whole cloves
A 2-inch piece fresh ginger (optional)
1 stick cinnamon
1½ cups (12 ounces) aquavit
1½ cups sugar
2 cups whole almonds, blanched and
    peeled

About 2 dozen mugs or punch cups

In a 6- to 8-quart enameled or stainless-steel pot, mix together the dry red wine, muscatel, sweet vermouth, bitters, raisins, orange peel and the spices: the slightly crushed cardamoms, whole cloves, ginger and cinnamon. Cover and let the mixture stand for at least 12 hours so that the flavors will develop and mingle. Shortly before serving, add the aquavit and the sugar. Stir well and bring to a full boil over high heat. Remove at once from the heat, stir in the almonds and serve the hot *glögg* in mugs. In Sweden, where this is a popular Christmas-season drink, a small spoon is placed in each mug to scoop up the almonds and raisins.

To make a simpler *glögg*, divide the quantities of spices in half and mix them with 2 bottles of dry red wine. Leave it overnight, then stir in ¾ cup of sugar and bring almost to a boil. Remove from the heat, stir in 1 cup of whole, blanched and peeled almonds, and serve hot.

—from THE COOKING OF SCANDINAVIA

Hot Buttered Rum
To make 1 hot drink

1½ teaspoons superfine sugar
A 1-inch piece cinnamon stick
3 ounces rum
1 cup hot milk
1 tablespoon unsalted butter
Ground nutmeg

A 12-ounce mug

Wash the mug with very hot water and shake it dry. Place the sugar, piece of cinnamon stick and rum in the mug, and stir to dissolve the sugar. Pour in the hot milk, top with the tablespoon of butter, and sprinkle with ground nutmeg.

Hot Toddy
To make 1 toddy

Pinch of superfine sugar
1 strip lemon peel stuck with 1
   whole clove
Pinch of cinnamon, or substitute a 1-
   inch piece cinnamon stick
3 ounces bourbon, blended whiskey
   or brandy
Boiling water

An old-fashioned glass or a 6- to 8-
   ounce mug

Warm the glass or mug by washing it with very hot water and shaking it dry. Place the pinch of sugar, lemon peel stuck with a clove, cinnamon and spirits in the glass or mug, fill with boiling water, and stir.
   The hot toddy is a very popular cold remedy, but there is a less familiar drink, known as the toddy, which is simply whiskey, ice cubes and a strip of lemon peel.

Irish Coffee I
To serve 2

4 strips orange peel
4 strips lemon peel
16 whole cloves
1 stick cinnamon
2 teaspoons superfine sugar
5 ounces Irish whiskey
1½ cups strong hot coffee
A dish of superfine or confectioners'
    sugar
¼ cup whipped heavy cream

Two 8-ounce stemmed goblets, mugs
    or cups

Stud the strips of orange and lemon peel with 2 cloves each and place them in a skillet or chafing dish with the stick of cinnamon and the 2 teaspoons of sugar. Set over moderate heat, stirring occasionally with a wooden spoon, until the sugar has melted; pour the Irish whiskey into the pan and light a match to the liquid. Be sure to step back since the flame will flare up instantly. Shake the pan back and forth slowly until the flame dies out; pour in the hot coffee all at once and let it come to a simmer. Remove from the heat.

Rub the cut edge of a strip of lemon peel around the inside of each glass or mug and dip the container into a dish of sugar so that the sugar adheres to the inside rim. Pour in the coffee, trying not to disturb the sugar. Top each serving with a dollop of whipped cream.

Irish Coffee II
To serve 1

1 teaspoon sugar
1½ ounces Irish whiskey
5 ounces strong, hot coffee
1 tablespoon whipped heavy cream

An 8-ounce stemmed goblet

This simpler version of Irish coffee is reputedly the original, made famous in the Buena Vista Café at San Francisco's Fisherman's Wharf after World War II.

Rinse the goblet with very hot water and shake it dry. Place the sugar in the glass, pour in the Irish whiskey and then the coffee, stir to dissolve the sugar, and top with whipped cream.

Tom and Jerry
To serve 2

¾ cup milk
2 tablespoons unsalted butter
2 eggs
2 teaspoons sugar
⅛ teaspoon vanilla extract
3 ounces brandy
3 ounces Jamaica rum
Ground nutmeg

Three 6- to 8-ounce mugs

Combine the milk and butter in a saucepan and place over low heat until the butter is melted and the milk is hot. Meanwhile, separate the eggs. Place the egg whites in a small bowl and beat them with a wire whisk or a rotary or electric beater until they are frothy. In another bowl, beat the yolks until they thicken slightly and are well combined. Pour the egg whites into the bowl with the yolks and beat in the sugar and vanilla.

Remove the milk from the heat and pour the eggs into the pan, whisking constantly. Return the pan to the heat, add the brandy and rum, and continue to whisk while the ingredients warm. Do not let them boil or the drink will curdle.

Pour about half of the contents of the pan into a mug, then pour back and forth from one mug to another to make sure the drink is well combined and froths. Continue pouring back and forth with the other 2 mugs until a second mug has been filled. Sprinkle the top of each drink with ground nutmeg and serve hot.

Vin Chaud (or Glühwein)

To serve 2

2 slices lemon
4 whole cloves
2 tablespoons superfine sugar
1½ sticks cinnamon
2 cups (1 pint) claret or Burgundy

Two 8-ounce mugs

Stud each lemon slice with 2 cloves and combine them with the sugar and cinnamon sticks in a 1-quart enameled, copper or stainless-steel skillet, casserole or chafing dish. Place over moderate heat, stir occasionally with a wooden spoon until the sugar has melted, then pour in the red wine. Continue to stir until the wine has almost reached the boiling point. Remove from the heat immediately, scoop out the lemon slices and cinnamon with a spoon or spatula, and pour the hot wine into mugs.

Hors d'Oeuvre and Canapés

The recipes in this part of the Recipe Booklet are for foods that go well with cocktails or apéritifs—many may be served, of course, as appetizers without drinks. Most of the recipes were developed and tested for this volume alone; a few have been selected from other volumes in the series and are included as a convenience.

Anchoyade
HOT ANCHOVY CANAPÉ

To serve 4 to 5

2 two-ounce cans flat anchovy fillets	Freshly ground black pepper
2 medium garlic cloves, finely chopped	8 to 10 slices fresh French bread
1 teaspoon tomato paste	(½- to ¾-inch slices)
1 to 1½ tablespoons olive oil	1 teaspoon finely chopped fresh
2 teaspoons lemon juice or red-wine vinegar	parsley

Drain the anchovies of all their oil and place them in a large mortar or heavy bowl with the garlic and the tomato paste. Mash with a pestle, wooden masher or wooden spoon until the mixture is a very smooth purée. Dribble the oil in, a few drops at a time, stirring constantly, until the mixture becomes thick and smooth like mayonnaise. Stir in the lemon juice and a few grindings of pepper.

Preheat the oven to 500°. Under the broiler, brown the bread lightly on one side. While the bread is warm, spread the untoasted, soft side with the anchovy mixture, pressing it into the bread with the back of a fork or spoon. Arrange the bread on a baking sheet and bake in the oven for 10 minutes. Sprinkle with parsley and serve at once.

NOTE: For less saltiness, after draining the anchovies soak them for 10 minutes in cold water and then pat them thoroughly dry with paper towels.
—*from* THE COOKING OF PROVINCIAL FRANCE

Bagna Cauda
HOT ANCHOVY AND GARLIC DIP

To serve 6

1 cucumber, peeled, seeded and cut
    into 2-by-½-inch strips
2 carrots, peeled and cut into
    2-by-½-inch strips
1 sweet red pepper, seeded and cut
    into 2-by-½-inch strips
1 green pepper, seeded and cut into
    2-by-½-inch strips
4 celery stalks, cut into 2-by-½-inch
    strips
1 bunch scallions, trimmed and cut
    into 2-inch lengths

A small head of romaine, broken into
    separate leaves
12 cherry tomatoes
¼ pound fresh mushrooms, whole if
    small, quartered if large
Italian bread sticks

2 cups heavy cream
4 tablespoons butter
8 flat anchovy fillets, drained, rinsed
    and finely chopped
1 teaspoon finely chopped garlic
1 canned white truffle, finely chopped
    (optional)

Soak the vegetable strips in a bowl of ice cubes and water for an hour to crisp them. Pat dry with paper towels and arrange on a platter with the romaine leaves, tomatoes and mushrooms. Cover with plastic wrap and refrigerate. Arrange the bread sticks on a separate plate and set aside.

In a heavy 1-quart enameled or stainless-steel saucepan, bring the cream to a boil and cook it, stirring frequently, for about 15 to 20 minutes, or until it has thickened and has reduced to about 1 cup.

Choose a 3- or 4-cup enameled or flameproof earthenware casserole that fits over a candle warmer, spirit lamp or electric hot tray. On the stove, melt the butter in the casserole over low heat; do not let it brown. Add the anchovies and garlic, then the reduced cream and the optional truffle, and bring the sauce to a simmer, stirring constantly. Do not let it boil. Serve the *bagna cauda* at once, accompanied by the cold vegetables and the bread sticks. To eat, pick up a vegetable or bread stick with your fingers and dip it into the hot sauce. If the butter and cream separate as the sauce stands, beat with a wire whisk. (You may substitute almost any raw vegetable you like for *bagna cauda*: fennel sticks, cauliflower or broccoli flowerets, white turnip wedges, or red or white radishes.)   —*from* THE COOKING OF ITALY

Baklazhannaya Ikra

POOR MAN'S CAVIAR

To make about 3 cups

1 large eggplant, about 2 pounds
1 cup finely chopped onions
6 tablespoons olive oil
½ cup finely chopped green pepper
1 teaspoon finely chopped garlic
2 large ripe tomatoes, peeled, seeded
  and finely chopped, or ¼ cup
  canned tomato purée

½ teaspoon sugar
2 teaspoons salt
Freshly ground black pepper
2 to 3 tablespoons lemon juice
Pumpernickel bread or sesame seed
  crackers

Preheat the oven to 425°. Bake the eggplant on a rack in the center of the oven for about an hour, turning it over once or twice until the eggplant is soft and its skin is charred and blistered.

Meanwhile, cook the onions in 4 tablespoons of the oil over moderate heat for 6 to 8 minutes until they are soft but not brown. Stir in the green pepper and garlic and cook, stirring occasionally, for 5 minutes longer. Scrape the entire contents of the skillet into a mixing bowl.

Remove the skin from the baked eggplant with a small sharp knife, then chop the eggplant finely, almost to a purée. Add it to the mixing bowl and stir in the tomatoes or tomato purée, the sugar, salt and a few grindings of black pepper. Mix together thoroughly. Heat the remaining oil in the skillet over moderate heat and pour in the eggplant mixture. Bring to a boil, stirring constantly, then turn the heat low, cover the skillet and simmer for about an hour. Remove the cover and cook an additional half hour, stirring frequently, until all the moisture in the pan has evaporated and the mixture is thick enough to hold its shape in a spoon. Stir in 2 tablespoons of the lemon juice and taste for seasoning, adding more salt, freshly ground black pepper and lemon juice to taste. Transfer the "caviar" to a mixing bowl and chill, covered with plastic wrap, until ready to serve. Spread on squares of pumpernickel bread or sesame seed crackers. —*from* THE COOKING OF THE SOVIET UNION AND POLAND

Caponata

COLD EGGPLANT APPETIZER

To make about 8 cups

2 pounds eggplant, peeled and cut into ½-inch cubes (about 8 cups)
Salt
½ cup olive oil
2 cups finely chopped celery
¾ cup finely chopped onions
⅓ cup wine vinegar mixed with 4 teaspoons sugar
3 cups drained canned Italian plum or whole-pack tomatoes

2 tablespoons tomato paste
6 large green olives, pitted, slivered and well-rinsed
2 tablespoons capers
4 flat anchovy fillets, well rinsed and pounded smooth with a mortar and pestle
Salt
Freshly ground black pepper
2 tablespoons pine nuts

Sprinkle the cubes of eggplant generously with salt and set them in a colander or large sieve over paper towels to drain. After about 30 minutes, pat the cubes dry with fresh paper towels and set them aside.

In a heavy 12- to 14-inch skillet, heat ¼ cup of the olive oil. Add the celery and cook over moderate heat, stirring frequently, for 10 minutes. Then stir in the onions and cook for another 8 to 10 minutes, or until the celery and onions are soft and lightly colored. With a slotted spoon, transfer them to a bowl. Pour the remaining ¼ cup of olive oil into the skillet and over high heat sauté the eggplant cubes in it, stirring and turning them constantly for about 8 minutes, or until they are lightly browned. Return the celery and onions to the skillet and stir in the vinegar and sugar, drained tomatoes, tomato paste, green olives, capers, anchovies, 2 teaspoons salt and a few grindings of pepper. Bring to a boil, reduce the heat, and simmer uncovered, stirring frequently, for about 15 minutes. Stir in the pine nuts. Now taste the mixture and season it with salt and pepper and a little extra vinegar if necessary. Transfer the *caponata* to a serving bowl and refrigerate it until ready to serve.   —*from* THE COOKING OF ITALY

Ćevapčići

SKEWERED LAMB-AND-BEEF SAUSAGE ROLLS

To serve 6

1 tablespoon lard
½ cup finely chopped onions
½ teaspoon finely chopped garlic
1 pound ground lamb
1 pound ground beef chuck

1 egg white, lightly beaten
1 teaspoon salt
1 tablespoon sweet Hungarian
   paprika
2 tablespoons lard (optional)
2 tablespoons very finely chopped
   onions

Heat the lard in an 8-inch skillet over high heat until a light haze forms over it. Reduce the heat to medium, add the onions and garlic and, stirring occasionally, cook them for 6 to 8 minutes, or until the onions are lightly colored. Scrape them into a large mixing bowl.

Add the lamb, beef, egg white, salt and paprika. Mix well with your hands or a wooden spoon.

Shape the mixture into small cylinders approximately 1 inch in diameter and 2 inches long and arrange them on a plate. Cover the plate with wax paper or plastic wrap and then refrigerate it for at least an hour before cooking, or until the meat mixture has become firm.

Arrange the cylinders on 6- to 10-inch metal skewers, 4 or 5 to a skewer, leaving at least ¼ inch space between them and running the skewers through the sides, not the ends, of the cylinders.

Like most other meats cooked on skewers (kabobs) this Yugoslav favorite can be cooked in one of three ways.

Broil the ćevapčići on a charcoal grill or in a preheated oven broiler that is 4 to 6 inches from the flame. Another method is to fry them over high heat in a heavy 12-inch skillet in which 2 tablespoons of lard have been heated to the smoking point. If the ćevapčići are broiled on a grill or in an oven broiler, cook them about 8 minutes on each side, or until they are dark brown on the outside and well done on the inside. If ćevapčići are cooked in a skillet, they should be turned every so often, a skewerful at a time, with a wide metal spatula.

Ćevapčići may be served on the skewers so that the diners may remove them or they may be removed from the skewers before serving. Sprinkle the meat sausage rolls with the finely chopped onion just before serving. Ćevapčići may also be served as a cocktail hors d'oeuvre. A spicy accompaniment to ćevapčići is tiny hot peppers.

—*from* THE COOKING OF VIENNA'S EMPIRE

Cheese Fondue

To serve 4

1 clove garlic, peeled	3 tablespoons flour
2 cups dry white wine, preferably Neuchâtel, Riesling or Chablis	Salt
1 teaspoon lemon juice	Freshly ground black pepper
1 pound grated or shredded imported Swiss cheese, or half Gruyère and half Emmentaler combined (about 4 cups)	Ground nutmeg (optional)
	2 tablespoons kirsch
	1 large loaf Italian or French bread, cut into 1-inch cubes, with crust

Vigorously rub the inside of a fondue pan, flameproof casserole or heavy chafing dish with the peeled clove of garlic. Pour in the wine and lemon juice, and over moderate direct heat, bring it almost to a boil. Mix the grated or shredded cheese with the flour. Then, handful by handful, drop in the cheese, stirring constantly with a fork. Continue to stir until the cheese melts into a thick cream. Season to taste with salt, a few gratings of black pepper and a little nutmeg, if you like the flavor. Stir in the kirsch and set the pot over a table warmer such as a fondue warmer, an alcohol burner or an electric hot plate. If you are using a chafing dish, set the pan over hot water. Regulate the heat so that the fondue simmers gently but does not boil.

To eat the fondue, spear a bread cube with a long-handled fork (there are special fondue forks available for this purpose), dip the bread into the simmering cheese mixture and twirl the bread to coat it evenly with the fondue. If the fondue becomes too thick as it simmers, thin it with heated wine stirred in by the tablespoonful.

Cheese Pennies

To make about 3 dozen

8 tablespoons butter (1 quarter-pound stick), softened	¾ cup sifted flour
½ pound Cheddar cheese, grated (about 2 cups)	½ teaspoon salt
	⅛ teaspoon cayenne
	½ teaspoon powdered mustard

Cream the butter by beating it against the sides of a bowl with a wooden spoon until it is light and fluffy. Then beat in the cheese. Still beating, add the flour, ¼ cup at a time, then the salt, cayenne and mustard. (The entire process may be done more easily in an electric mixer equipped with a paddle or pastry arm attachment.) In either case, the mixture should be dense enough to be formed into a compact ball. If it is too soft to hold together, beat in additional flour by the tablespoonful, testing the dough for density after each addition. On a lightly floured surface, shape the ball into a sausagelike roll about 10 inches long and 1¼ inches wide, wrap it in wax paper and refrigerate for at least an hour, until firm.

Preheat the oven to 350°. With a sharp, thin knife, carefully slice the chilled dough into ¼-inch rounds and arrange them ½ inch apart on an ungreased cookie sheet. Bake in the middle of the oven for 8 to 10 minutes, or until the pennies are firm and golden brown. Watch carefully; they burn easily. Transfer them with a metal spatula to a rack to cool. The cheese pennies may be served at once at room temperature, or stored in an airtight container or frozen for future use.

Chicken Salad Sandwiches
To make 16 sandwiches

1 cup finely chopped freshly cooked or canned chicken
2 tablespoons finely chopped celery
1 tablespoon grated onion
½ teaspoon curry powder
½ teaspoon salt

Freshly ground black pepper
1 cup mayonnaise, freshly made, or a good unsweetened commercial variety
4 thin slices white bread
4 thin slices pumpernickel bread
1 cup finely chopped toasted almonds

Combine the chicken, celery, grated onion, curry powder, salt and a few grindings of black pepper in a bowl and mix thoroughly. Add ¼ cup of mayonnaise and mix again. If the mixture seems too dry, add another tablespoon of the mayonnaise. Taste for seasoning.

Cut away the crusts from the white and pumpernickel breads and trim the 8 slices to the same size. Spread each slice of bread with a thin coating of mayonnaise and divide the chicken salad mixture evenly on the four slices of white bread. Top with the pumpernickel slices and cut each sandwich into 4 squares, rectangles or triangles. Dip the outer edges of each sandwich in the remaining mayonnaise, then into the chopped almonds, pressing them firmly to make the almonds adhere. Arrange the sandwiches attractively on a large platter, cover with plastic wrap and refrigerate until ready to serve.

Funghi Marinati
MARINATED MUSHROOMS

To make about 2 cups

2/3 cup olive oil
1/2 cup water
Juice of about 2 lemons
1 bay leaf

2 garlic cloves, bruised with the flat
    of a knife
6 whole peppercorns
1/2 teaspoon salt
1 pound small whole fresh
    mushrooms

Combine the 2/3 cup of olive oil, 1/2 cup of water, juice of 2 lemons, bay leaf, bruised garlic cloves, peppercorns and salt in a 10- to 12-inch enameled or stainless-steel skillet, and bring to a boil over moderate heat. Reduce the heat, cover and simmer for 15 minutes. Strain this marinade through a sieve and return it to the skillet; bring to a simmer over low heat. Drop the mushrooms into the marinade and simmer, turning them over from time to time, for 5 minutes.

Let the mushrooms cool in the marinade. Serve them at room temperature or, after they have cooled, refrigerate them and serve them cold. (The mushrooms will keep in the refrigerator at least 2 days.) Before serving, lift the mushrooms out of the marinade with a slotted spoon, draining them carefully, and arrange them on a platter or in a serving bowl. Serve as part of an antipasto. —*from* THE COOKING OF ITALY

Gefüllte Gurken
CUCUMBERS STUFFED WITH HAM AND SOUR PICKLES

To serve 6 to 8

2 cucumbers, 6 to 8 inches long
1/2 teaspoon salt
2 boneless sardines
1/4 pound boiled ham, diced
2 hard-cooked eggs, coarsely
    chopped

2 teaspoons finely chopped onions
2 tablespoons minced sour pickles
1 teaspoon prepared French mustard
2 to 4 tablespoons mayonnaise,
    freshly made or a good commercial
    brand

Cut 1/2 inch off the tip of each cucumber, then peel the cucumbers with a vegetable scraper or sharp knife. Cut out the seeds and center pulp with a long iced-tea spoon, leaving a shell about 1/4 inch thick. Pour 1/4 teaspoon of salt into each cucumber, rubbing it in as evenly as possible with your forefinger, let the cucumber shells stand for about 15 minutes, then thoroughly dry them inside with a piece of paper toweling.

In a medium-sized mixing bowl, mash the sardines to a paste with a fork or wooden spoon. Add the ham, eggs, onions, pickles, mustard and 2 tablespoons of mayonnaise. Stir the ingredients together until the mixture holds its shape in a spoon. (If it seems too dry, add more mayonnaise.) Taste for seasoning. The amount of salt needed will depend on the saltiness of the sardines and ham.

Stuff the cucumbers by standing them on end and spooning the filling in, tamping it down with a spoon as you proceed. When they are all tightly packed, wrap them separately in wax paper or aluminum foil and refrigerate them for 2 hours, or until the filling is firm.

To serve, slice the cucumbers crosswise, on a slant, in slices about ½ inch thick.   —*from* THE COOKING OF VIENNA'S EMPIRE

Guacamole
AVOCADO DIP

To make about 3 cups

2 large ripe avocados	and coarsely chopped (about ½ cup)
1 tablespoon finely chopped onion	1 tablespoon finely chopped fresh coriander
2 canned serrano chilies, drained, washed and finely chopped	½ teaspoon salt
2 medium tomatoes, peeled, seeded	Freshly ground black pepper

Peel the avocados, cut them in half and discard the pits. Chop the avocados coarsely; then, in a large mixing bowl, mash with a fork to a smooth purée. (If you prefer a finer texture, rub the fruit through a sieve with the back of a large spoon.) Add the chopped onions, chilies, tomato, coriander, salt and a few grindings of black pepper and mix together thoroughly. Taste for seasoning. To prevent the *guacamole* from darkening, cover it with plastic wrap or foil and refrigerate until ready to use. Serve as a dip with crisp tortillas or crackers.

—*from* THE COOKING OF LATIN AMERICA

Ham Balls

To make 32 ham balls

1 cup fresh bread crumbs

3 tablespoons milk

1 pound fresh lean pork, finely ground, combined with ½ pound cooked smoked ham, finely ground

1 tablespoon prepared mustard

1 tablespoon finely chopped fresh parsley

1 egg, lightly beaten

Freshly ground black pepper

2 tablespoons butter

2 tablespoons vegetable oil

¾ cup dry red wine

Soak the bread crumbs in the milk for about 5 minutes, then combine them with the ground pork and ham in a large mixing bowl. Add the mustard, parsley, lightly beaten egg and a few grindings of black pepper, and with a large spoon mix them thoroughly together. Form the mixture into small balls about 1 inch in diameter and chill for at least ½ hour.

Preheat the oven to 350°. Over high heat, melt the butter with the oil in a large, heavy skillet. When the foam subsides, add the ham balls. To help keep their shape as they brown, roll the balls around in the hot fat by shaking the pan back and forth over the burner. When the ham balls are well browned on all sides (this should take about 5 minutes), transfer them with a slotted spoon to a 2-quart casserole. Pour off all but a thin film of fat from the skillet and pour in the wine. Bring it to a boil over high heat, scraping and stirring into it any brown bits clinging to the bottom and sides of the pan. Cook briskly for about a minute, then pour the wine into the casserole. Cover tightly and bake in the middle of the oven for about 30 minutes, basting the ham balls after 15 minutes with the wine. Serve either directly from the casserole or arrange the balls on a heated platter and pour the sauce over them. Or, place the ham balls and sauce in a chafing dish and serve, speared with decorative tooth picks, as an accompaniment to cocktails. —*from* AMERICAN COOKING

Humus

CHICK-PEA SPREAD

To make 3 cups

2 cups cooked chick-peas *(garbanzos)*,
    freshly cooked or canned
1½ teaspoons salt
3 cloves garlic, finely chopped

½ to ¾ cup vegetable oil
¼ cup fresh lemon juice
2 tablespoons coarsely chopped
    parsley, flat-leaf type preferably, or
    2 tablespoons chopped mint

If the chick-peas are canned, drain them through a sieve and wash them under cold running water until the water runs clear. Spread them on paper towels and pat them dry. Freshly cooked chick-peas need only be drained and cooled.

To make the *humus* in a blender, place the chick-peas, salt, garlic, ½ cup of oil and ¼ cup of lemon juice in the container and blend at high speed for 10 seconds. Stop the blender and scrape down the sides with a rubber spatula. Blend again at high speed, adding as much oil as you need to prevent the blender from clogging. The finished *humus* should be a very smooth purée, just thick enough to hold its shape in a spoon. Taste for seasoning and add more salt and lemon juice if you like.

To make the *humus* by hand, force the chick-peas through a sieve with the back of a large spoon or purée them in a food mill. Add the salt and garlic and, beating constantly, slowly pour in as much oil and lemon juice as necessary to form a smooth, thick purée. Taste for seasoning.

Transfer the *humus* to a serving dish and sprinkle it with the parsley or mint. Serve this Middle Eastern spread on pieces of flat Arabic bread, if available, or on sesame seed crackers.

—*from* THE COOKING OF THE MIDDLE EAST

Liptovský Sýr
LIPTAUER CHEESE

To make approximately 2 cups

8 ounces cottage cheese
8 tablespoons (1 quarter-pound stick)
   unsalted butter, softened
1 tablespoon sweet Hungarian
   paprika
Freshly ground black pepper

¼ teaspoon salt
2 teaspoons caraway seeds
1 teaspoon dry mustard
1 teaspoon chopped capers
1 tablespoon finely chopped onions
½ cup sour cream (plus ¼ cup if a
   dip is desired)
3 tablespoons finely chopped chives

With a wooden spoon rub the cottage cheese through a sieve into a mixing bowl. Cream the butter by beating it against the side of a mixing bowl with a wooden spoon. Beat in the cheese, the paprika, a generous grinding of black pepper, the salt, caraway seeds, mustard, capers, onions and sour cream.

Continue beating vigorously with a wooden spoon or by using an electric mixer at medium speed until the mixture forms a smooth paste.

If the Liptauer cheese is to be used as a spread, shape it into a mound and decorate it with the chives, or shape it into a ball that may be rolled in the chives. Refrigerate it for 2 hours, or until it is firm.

To make a Liptauer dip, stir the extra sour cream into the paste with a wooden spoon or beat it in with an electric mixer. Sprinkle the chives over the dip after it has been poured into a serving bowl.

—from THE COOKING OF VIENNA'S EMPIRE

Mushroom Caps Stuffed with Anchovy Cream Cheese
To make 3 dozen

36 small white mushrooms, each
   about 1 inch in diameter (about 1
   pound)
An 8-ounce package of cream cheese,

   softened to room temperature
2 tablespoons anchovy paste
1 teaspoon lemon juice
1 teaspoon finely grated onion
2 tablespoons finely cut fresh chives

One at a time, remove the stems from the mushrooms by holding their caps securely, and gently bending back the stems until they snap free. With a small sharp knife, cut away any part of the stem that adheres to the center of the mushroom. It is not necessary to wash the mushrooms; merely wipe them clean with a damp cloth.

In a small mixing bowl, beat the cream cheese with a large spoon until smooth. Beat in the anchovy paste, lemon juice and grated onion. Taste for seasoning. Then spoon the mixture into a pastry bag fitted with a small star tip and pipe it into the mushroom caps. Or, if you prefer, use a small spoon to fill the mushrooms with the cheese mixture, mounding it slightly. Sprinkle lightly with the chives and refrigerate the mushrooms until ready to serve.

New Potatoes with Sour Cream and Caviar
To make 12 hors d'oeuvre

12 unpeeled new potatoes, 1 to 1½ inches in diameter, thoroughly scrubbed	onions or scallions
	Freshly ground black pepper
	¾ cup sour cream
Salt	1 tablespoon black caviar
1 to 2 tablespoons finely chopped	1 tablespoon finely chopped parsley

Drop the potatoes into a 2-quart saucepan of boiling water. Over moderate heat, cook them uncovered for 15 to 20 minutes, or until they offer no resistance when pierced with the tip of a sharp knife. Drain immediately, and pat the potatoes dry with paper towels.

With a melon scoop or teaspoon, neatly scoop out about ⅓ of each potato, and sprinkle the opening lightly with salt. Then fill with about ¼ teaspoon of the chopped onions or scallions, a few grindings of black pepper and about 1 tablespoon of the sour cream, or a little less than the cavities will hold. Top with about ¼ teaspoon of caviar and sprinkle with a little chopped parsley. Serve warm.

Oyster Fritters

To serve 4 to 6

1 cup flour
½ teaspoon salt
1 tablespoon melted butter
1 egg, lightly beaten
½ cup beer

2 dozen fresh oysters, shucked, or 2
  dozen frozen oysters, thoroughly
  defrosted
1 egg white
Vegetable shortening or vegetable oil
  for deep-fat frying
Lemon wedges

Sift ½ cup of the flour and the salt into a mixing bowl. With a wooden spoon stir in the butter and the egg. Then pour in the beer gradually and mix only until the batter is fairly smooth. Don't overmix. Let the batter rest at room temperature for about an hour. When you are ready to fry the oysters, beat the egg white with a rotary beater or whisk until it is stiff enough to form unwavering peaks on the beater when it is lifted out of the bowl. Gently fold the beaten egg white into the batter and continue to fold until no streaks of white remain.

In a deep-fat fryer, heat the shortening or oil until it registers 375° on a deep-frying thermometer. The fat should be at least 3 inches deep. Dip the oysters in the remaining ½ cup of flour, shake off any excess and then dip in the batter. Let the excess batter drain off, then fry the oysters, 5 or 6 at a time, for 3 to 4 minutes until they are puffed and golden brown. Drain on paper towels and keep the fritters warm in a 200° oven until all the oysters have been fried. Serve at once with wedges of lemon.

—*from* AMERICAN COOKING

Parslied Onion Sandwiches

To make 36 sandwiches

1 loaf fresh homemade-type white
  bread, unsliced
1 cup mayonnaise, freshly made, or
  a good unsweetened commercial
  variety

1 large Bermuda onion or 2 to 3 red
  onions, peeled and sliced into
  paper-thin rounds
Salt
Freshly ground black pepper
1 cup very finely chopped parsley

With a large serrated knife, cut 18 slices of bread about ⅛ inch thick. Place the slices side by side and spread each slice with a thin coating of mayonnaise. Arrange a single layer of the onion slices on half the bread slices, sprinkle them with salt and a few grindings of black pepper and top with the remaining slices of bread. With a 1½-inch cookie cutter, firmly cut 4 rounds out of each sandwich, avoiding the crusts. Roll the cut edges of each sandwich like cartwheels in the remaining mayonnaise. Then roll the sandwich rounds similarly in the chopped parsley, pressing them in the parsley firmly enough to make a light coating adhere. Cover with plastic wrap and refrigerate the sandwiches until ready to serve.

Scallops Remoulade
To serve 4 to 6

1½ to 2 pounds fresh bay scallops

Only very fresh, tiny bay scallops can be served raw successfully. (Frozen and defrosted ones will not do.) Wash the scallops quickly under cold running water and dry them thoroughly with paper towels. Chill until ready to serve.

REMOULADE SAUCE

1 cup mayonnaise, freshly made, or a good unsweetened commercial variety
1 teaspoon dry mustard
1 teaspoon lemon juice
¼ to ½ teaspoon garlic, finely chopped
1 tablespoon capers, drained, washed and finely chopped
1 tablespoon fresh tarragon, finely chopped, or 2 teaspoons finely crumbled dried tarragon
1 tablespoon finely chopped parsley
1 hard-cooked egg, finely chopped
Salt
Cayenne or Tabasco

For the remoulade sauce, combine the mayonnaise, dry mustard and lemon juice in a small mixing bowl. Stir in the chopped garlic, capers, tarragon, parsley and hard-cooked egg. Mix together gently but thoroughly, and season to taste with salt and a few grains of cayenne pepper or drops of Tabasco. Arrange the scallops, pierced with decorative picks, on a chilled serving plate and pass the remoulade sauce separately.

—*from* AMERICAN COOKING

Steak Tartare Balls

To make about 2 dozen

1 pound ground top round beef, free
   of all fat, and of the best quality
1 tablespoon Worcestershire sauce
½ teaspoon salt

Freshly ground black pepper
¼ cup finely chopped chives, or the
   green stems of scallions, finely
   chopped
2 tablespoons (1 ounce) black caviar

In a small mixing bowl, thoroughly combine the beef, Worcestershire sauce, ½ teaspoon of salt and a few grindings of pepper. Taste for seasoning, then shape the mixture into balls about 1 inch in diameter. Make a small indentation in each ball with the tip of a small spoon or your finger, and one by one, roll the balls in the chopped chives or scallions so that the herbs adhere to the surface of the meat. Fill the indentations of each ball with about ¼ teaspoon of caviar, arrange them caviar side up on an attractive platter and chill before serving.

    More easily, if less impressively, the steak balls may be served without the caviar, in which case simply roll the balls in the herbs without indenting them.

Tapanade

BLACK OLIVE, ANCHOVY AND TUNA DIP

To make approximately 2 cups

3 two-ounce cans flat anchovy fillets,
   drained
A 7-ounce can tuna fish, drained
A 7-ounce can black pitted olives, if
   possible the imported
   Mediterranean type

¼ cup capers, thoroughly drained
4 medium cloves garlic, coarsely
   chopped
⅓ cup lemon juice
¼ to ½ cup olive oil
1 teaspoon freshly ground black
   pepper

If you have an electric blender, use it to make the *tapanade*—it is the quickest and easiest way to prepare this piquant vegetable dip from the South of France. Place in the jar of the blender the anchovies, the tuna fish, olives, capers, garlic and lemon juice. Blend at medium speed for about 2 minutes, stopping the blender after every 30 seconds to scrape down the sides of the jar with a rubber spatula. Continue to blend until the mixture becomes a smooth purée. With a rubber spatula, scrape it into a small mixing bowl. Using a wire whisk or wooden spoon, beat into it the olive oil, a tablespoon at a time, until ¼ cup of the oil has been absorbed. The *tapanade* should hold its shape lightly in a spoon. If it doesn't, beat in the remaining oil by tablespoons until it reaches the proper consistency. Stir in the black pepper and taste for seasoning, adding more pepper if you prefer the *tapanade* more highly seasoned.

To make the *tapanade* by hand, chop the anchovy fillets, tuna fish, olives, capers and garlic as finely as possible, and combine them by beating them together vigorously with a spoon for 2 or 3 minutes in a medium-sized bowl. Beat in the lemon juice and then the olive oil, using as much of it as you need to achieve the consistency described above. Season the *tapanade* as above.

VEGETABLES

1 sweet red pepper and 1 green pepper, cut into strips 2 to 3 inches long and ½ inch wide
2 to 3 medium carrots, scraped and cut into strips 2 to 3 inches long and ½ inch wide
2 to 3 stalks celery, cut into strips 2 to 3 inches long and ½ inch wide
8 to 12 whole red radishes
8 to 12 scallions, well trimmed

Although the vegetable strips may be served with the dip without any further preparation, they will be crisper if they are first soaked in ice water for about an hour and then thoroughly dried. Vegetables other than the ones listed may also be used: small raw mushrooms, raw broccoli or cauliflower flowerettes, strips of raw turnips, or endive spears.

If stored in airtight jars in the refrigerator, the *tapanade* will keep almost indefinitely.

Taramasalata

CARP ROE SPREAD

To make 1 cup

8 thin slices white bread, crusts
    removed
1 cup cold water
A 10-ounce jar *tarama* (salted carp
    roe)

¼ cup lemon juice
2 tablespoons finely grated onion
½ cup olive oil
2 tablespoons finely chopped parsley
12 small black olives, preferably the
    Mediterranean type

Soak the bread in the cold water for about 5 minutes, then with your hands squeeze it thoroughly dry. To make the *taramasalata* with an electric mixer, combine the bread and *tarama* in the mixing bowl and beat at medium speed until the mixture is smooth and pastelike. Still beating, add the grated onion, lemon juice and then the oil, 1 tablespoon at a time. When all the oil has been absorbed, the *taramasalata* should have the consistency of a thick mayonnaise.

To make by hand, pound the squeezed bread with a wooden pestle in a mortar until it is smooth. As you proceed, add the *tarama*, a teaspoon or so at a time, and then the onion and the lemon juice. Transfer this pasty mixture to a bowl, and with a wooden spoon, whisk or rotary beater, beat in the olive oil as described above.

To serve, spread the *taramasalata* in a mound on a serving plate, sprinkle it with the chopped parsley and surround it with the black olives. Serve as a spread with sesame seed or other crisp crackers.

—*from* THE COOKING OF THE MIDDLE EAST

Tomato Cheese Croustades

To make 12 *croustades*

1 tablespoon soft butter
12 thin slices fresh white bread
1 small tomato, peeled, seeded and
   coarsely chopped (about 2
   tablespoons)
1 teaspoon fresh basil, finely chopped

or ½ teaspoon dried, crumbled basil
½ teaspoon salt
Freshly ground black pepper
¼ cup grated Swiss cheese, preferably
   Gruyère
2 tablespoons butter, cut into ¼-inch
   bits

Preheat the oven to 400°. To make the little bread cases called *croustades*, you will need a muffin tin composed of 12 tiny cups, each about 2 inches in diameter. With a pastry brush, lightly coat each cup with the soft butter. Cut 2½-inch rounds from the centers of the bread slices using a cookie cutter or the rim of a wine glass. Fit the rounds in the tins, molding them gently to form little cups. Don't fuss with them too much. Bake the *croustades* in the middle of the oven for 10 to 12 minutes until golden brown, then remove them from the tin and cool. The *croustades* may be prepared as much as a day in advance, or a large supply may be frozen for later use.

Fill the *croustades* just before baking or hours earlier, if you wish. Preheat the oven to 400°. In a small bowl, combine the tomato, basil, salt and a few grindings of black pepper, and taste for seasoning. Fill each *croustade* with 1 teaspoon of grated cheese and spread about ½ teaspoon of the tomato mixture on top. Then dot with butter. Arrange the *croustades* on a cookie sheet or jelly-roll pan and bake for about 10 minutes. Slide under the broiler for a few seconds to brown the tops, and serve hot.

Terrine Maison

HOME-STYLE PÂTÉ

To serve 10 to 12

1 pound fresh pork fat, ground
1½ pounds lean pork, ground
1½ pounds calf's, beef or pork liver,
    ground
½ pound lean veal, ground
5 tablespoons butter
⅓ cup finely chopped shallots or
    scallions
½ teaspoon finely chopped garlic
½ pound whole chicken livers
¼ cup cognac
3 tablespoons heavy cream

2 teaspoons lemon juice
2 tablespoons flour
1 egg, lightly beaten
½ teaspoon spice Parisienne or
    allspice
1½ tablespoons salt
Freshly ground black pepper
¼ pound cooked smoked beef tongue
    or baked ham cut in ¼- inch cubes
    (about 1 cup) (optional)
½ pound fresh pork fat back, the fat
    from a pork loin or fat salt pork,
    sliced into ⅛-inch strips or sheets
1 large bay leaf

Combine the ground meats in a large mixing bowl. In a heavy 8- to 10-inch skillet, melt 3 tablespoons of butter over moderate heat. When the foam subsides, stir in the shallots and garlic and cook, stirring frequently, for 5 minutes, or until soft but not brown. With a spatula, scrape into the bowl of meat.

In the same skillet, melt 2 tablespoons of butter and cook the chicken livers for 3 or 4 minutes or until they have stiffened but are still pink inside. Remove the livers with a slotted spoon and set them aside on a plate. Pour the cognac into the hot skillet and boil it, stirring and scraping in any browned bits that cling to the bottom or sides of the pan, until it has reduced to about 2 tablespoons. Pour this glaze over the meat and shallots. Set the skillet aside.

Add the cream, lemon juice, flour, egg, spice Parisienne or allspice, salt and a generous grinding of pepper to the meat mixture. Knead vigorously with both hands, then beat with a wooden spoon (or in an electric beater with a pastry arm) until all the ingredients are well blended and the mixture is smooth and fluffy. Lightly fold in the tongue or ham cubes if they are used. Because the mixture contains raw pork, sauté a spoonful of it in the waiting skillet before tasting it for seasoning. Add more seasoning then if needed.

Preheat the oven to 350° and line a deep, rectangular 2-quart mold which has a cover (a *terrine*, or a metal or glass baking pan) with thin strips or sheets of pork fat. Depending on their length, the strips may be arranged lengthwise or crosswise, but they should overlap slightly and completely cover the bottom and sides of the mold. If they are long enough, let them hang over the sides and later lap them back over the top of the filling; otherwise, save enough strips of the fat to cover the top of the *terrine*.

Spoon half of the meat mixture into the lined mold, pressing it down firmly and smoothing it with the back of the spoon or a rubber spatula. Cut the chicken livers into quarters or eighths, depending on their size, and lay them in a row down the center of the mold. Fill the mold with the remaining meat mixture.

Smooth the top with a spoon or spatula and bring the long strips of fat from the sides up over the meat or arrange additional strips over it. Lay a bay leaf on the fat, enclose the top of the mold snugly with foil, then cover tightly.

Place the mold in a large baking pan on the middle shelf of the oven. Pour in enough boiling water to reach at least halfway up the side of the mold and bake the *terrine* for 2 hours or until the fat and juices which will have risen to the top are clear yellow.

Remove the *terrine* from the oven and lift off the cover and aluminum foil. Loosely cover the mold with fresh foil and weight the *terrine* by placing a heavy pan, casserole or cutting board, weighing at least several pounds, on top of it. Let cool to room temperature, then refrigerate the *terrine*, with the weight still in place, until it is thoroughly chilled. To serve, remove the weight and the foil, and cut slices directly from the mold in which the *terrine* baked.

—*from* THE COOKING OF PROVINCIAL FRANCE

Vårsmörgåsar
SPRING SANDWICHES

Makes 6 sandwiches or 24 hors d'oeuvre

½ loaf day-old homemade-type white
  bread, unsliced
10 anchovy fillets, finely chopped
4 tablespoons softened butter
2 tablespoons prepared Dijon mustard

4 hard-cooked eggs, finely chopped
¼ cup finely chopped dill, or ¼ cup
  combined dill, parsley and chives
⅛ teaspoon freshly ground black
  pepper
2 tablespoons butter
2 tablespoons vegetable oil

Trim the crusts from the loaf of bread and cut it into 12 slices ⅛ inch thick. In a small bowl, mash together the chopped anchovies, butter, mustard, eggs, herbs and pepper. The mixture should be quite smooth. Thickly spread it on 6 slices of bread. Top each slice with another piece of bread, and lightly press them together. At this point, the sandwiches may be wrapped in wax paper and refrigerated for up to 3 days or even frozen (they should be thoroughly defrosted before using).

Over moderate heat, melt the butter and oil in a 10- to 12-inch skillet. When the foam subsides, add the sandwiches, 2 or 3 at a time, and fry for 2 to 3 minutes on each side, until they are crisp and golden brown. Drain on paper towels and serve while hot, either whole as a main luncheon course or a snack, or cut in quarters to accompany cocktails.

—*from* THE COOKING OF SCANDINAVIA

Vegetables with Red Caviar Dip

To make 3 cups

VEGETABLES

4 cucumbers, peeled, seeded and cut
  into 2-by-½-inch strips
4 carrots, peeled and cut into 2-by-
  ½-inch strips

2 green peppers, seeded and cut into
  2-by-½-inch strips
4 celery stalks, cut into 2-by-½-inch
  strips
1 bunch scallions, trimmed and cut
  into 2-inch lengths
12 cherry tomatoes

Soak the vegetable strips in a bowl of ice water for an hour to crisp
them. Pat dry with paper towels and arrange on a platter with the tomatoes. Cover with plastic wrap and refrigerate.

VEGETABLE DIP

1 pint sour cream
2 tablespoons finely chopped fresh
  dill
2 tablespoons finely chopped

scallions, green stems only
½ teaspoon lemon juice
Pinch of cayenne pepper
8 ounces red caviar
1 tablespoon finely chopped parsley

Combine in a deep, attractive bowl the sour cream, dill, parsley,
chopped scallions, lemon juice and cayenne. Gently fold in the caviar
with a rubber spatula without crushing the fragile eggs. Taste for seasoning, then chill until ready to serve.

Serve cold, accompanied by the platter of cold vegetables.

Recipe Index

Whiskey

Gin

Vodka

Rum

Brandies and Liqueurs

Wines

Punches and Party Drinks

Hot Drinks

Hors d'Oeuvre and Canapés

Notes

Illustrations by Matt Greene
Drink recipes tested under the supervision of André Gros-Daillon   x